**The Creation of a
for School Leade**

The Creation of a Professional Learning Community for School Leaders

Insights on the Change Process from the Lens of the School Leader

Amalia Humada-Ludeke

SENSE PUBLISHERS
ROTTERDAM/BOSTON/TAIPEI

A C.I.P. record for this book is available from the Library of Congress.

ISBN: 978-94-6209-318-8 (paperback)
ISBN: 978-94-6209-319-5 (hardback)
ISBN: 978-94-6209-320-1 (e-book)

Published by: Sense Publishers,
P.O. Box 21858,
3001 AW Rotterdam,
The Netherlands
https://www.sensepublishers.com/

Printed on acid-free paper

All Rights Reserved © 2013 Sense Publishers

No part of this work may be reproduced, stored in a retrieval system, or transmitted in any form or by any means, electronic, mechanical, photocopying, microfilming, recording or otherwise, without written permission from the Publisher, with the exception of any material supplied specifically for the purpose of being entered and executed on a computer system, for exclusive use by the purchaser of the work.

TABLE OF CONTENTS

Acknowledgments	vii
Introduction	1
1 The Evolving Role of the Principal	13
2 University-District Partnerships	27
3 Developing the Model for the Administrators' PLC	43
4 Insights on the Principals Prior to the PLC	81
5 Changed Principal Perceptions	93
6 Impact on Practice	103
7 Principals' Perceptions of the University-District Partnership	115
8 Narrative from the Lens of the Author: A Compelling Purpose for This Project	131
Bibliography	149
Index	155

ACKNOWLEDGMENTS

I have been very privileged to have had the sustained opportunity to work with dedicated and hard-working school principals and administrators. I have forged relationships that have enriched both my life and practice. I have learned much from the experiences and perspectives of these steadfast school leaders who are deeply vested in attaining the best learning outcomes for the students whom they serve. I am grateful for the Alliance at the university who supported my vision to carry out an area of research that I felt compelled to study. Without the individual and collective efforts of both the university and public school district, representing two systems, the emergent collaboration could not have developed into a partnership. I am grateful for the leadership and unwavering support of the public school district partner, José E. Carrillo, Associate Superintendent. Without his leadership and collaborative efforts, the sustained 5-year university-district partnership would not have been possible.

INTRODUCTION

PURPOSE

The idea for this book emerged when an unexpected opportunity between a university and district partnership occurred. The university initiative known as the Alliance became the conduit for the initial collaboration between the two institutions. Building upon the tenets of an emerging theory in an area where little research has been conducted, I was compelled to explore the prospect of an innovative approach for addressing the existing problem of how professional development is historically delivered to school districts, and more specifically, to site-based principals. I was interested in exploring how principals may respond to receiving sustained, job-embedded professional development, focused on building leadership capacity.

The prolonged work between the two institutions, served to strengthen the partnership and cultivate a shared vision and common purpose. The participation and willingness of the dedicated and visionary leaders within the collaboration made it possible to further understand the processes gleaned from the participatory experiences of the principals, which served to build upon an emerging theory that has implications for practice, policy, and further research.

The author as researcher pursued the further exploration of the problem facing many of today's school principals, who are responsible for leading school improvement efforts, in an era of perpetual accountability. Many site-based principals are charged with implementing whole-school reform models designed to bring about significant change within the context of the organizational school culture. However, many of these leaders may not have the current ability to facilitate whole-school reform models (McDougall, Saunders, & Goldenberg, 2007) designed to transform a school culture, without having experienced the learning embedded in the change process and without having provided evidence of their own professional growth.

The researcher was interested in exploring the "under-researched topic" (Rowlands, 2005) centered on gleaning principals' perceptions through their lived-experiences of engaging in job-embedded professional development. The intent of the researcher was to build theory, through qualitative data collection (Rowlands, 2005), for the development of a model that could be advanced and refined over time. The researcher felt compelled to purposefully explore how and in what ways principals construct meaning of their change process when they were provided with the type of learning that reflects the tenets embedded in the models they are held accountable for implementing.

The emphasis in this research was placed on learning the processes and meanings of what the principals experienced throughout their participation in a sustained professional development model intended to build leadership capacity that embodies the tenets of how the role of the principalship is now defined. The researcher placed a strong focus on the interpretation of how principals understood the context of

INTRODUCTION

their constructed reality (Rowlands, 2005), and how they made meaning of the job-embedded professional development attained through the implementation of the model.

The author of this book, representing her institution of higher education, partnered together to leverage an opportunity that would lead to building leadership capacity of the stakeholders who participated in this project. This book unveiled the journey and told the story of the partnership and the remarkable principals who willingly participated in this project. Without the individual and collective contributions of the associate superintendent and the principals, this sustained partnership would not be possible.

The author strived to capture the story of the principals and the complex transformational process of the cohesive efforts reflected in this project. The commitment to stay together throughout the years when stakes were high revealed the rare level of allegiance forged between two institutions with differing priorities and perspectives.

RATIONALE FOR THE PROJECT

Historically, educational reform efforts have focused on teacher professional development. In an era of reform centered on accountability, instructional leadership, and student achievement, principals are increasingly charged in leading school improvement efforts. Research increasingly correlates the role of the school principal and student achievement, second to the role of the teacher (Hargreaves & Fink, 2003, Sergiovanni, 2009). Many of these leaders may not have had the necessary preparation to meet the demands of increasing student achievement which is entailed in a system-wide approach.

This project endeavored to address the gaps in knowledge related to instructional leadership and focus on the development of principals through the university-district partnership. The format of the training was influenced by the author representing the university, who wanted to develop a professional learning community of principals as a platform to provide sustained professional development. While some research exists related to the development of professional learning communities (DuFour, R. & DuFour, R. Eaker, & Many, 2006), most studies centered on learning communities have focused on the development of teachers. The scant research on gleaning principals' voices as learners in professional learning communities provided an opportunity to expound our collective knowledge on this under-researched topic.

THEORETICAL FRAMEWORKS

As an educator who has served in various professional capacities for over 30 years, I have developed strong core-beliefs and values. Irrefutably, these values, beliefs, and core assumptions have served to shape the lens in which I perceive the world, and thus respond to it. Several theories, models and frameworks have been purposeful

INTRODUCTION

in challenging my assumptions, while confirming others. The complex process of making meaning influenced by intrinsic and extrinsic forces have conclusively shaped who I am, and who I may still become.

FOUR FRAMEWORK APPROACH TO LEADERSHIP

For the purpose of guiding this 5-year project, two theoretical frameworks were of specific significance. The first Theoretical Framework which guided this project is the Four Framework Approach to Leadership developed by Bolman and Deal (1997, cited in Bolman & Deal, 2002). This framework is comprised of four frames (Bolman and Deal, 1997 in Bolman & Deal, 2002): the political frame; the human resource frame; the structural frame; and the symbolic frame. In addressing leadership challenges, Bolman and Deal (2002) presented the idea that the use of four frames is optimal for navigating the educational landscape. However, they also suggested, that most educators primarily rely on the human resource or structural lens (Bolman & Deal, 2002).

HUMAN RESOURCE FRAME

As I continue to develop and progress, I have become more adept at integrating the four frames. Without uncertainty, the principles embedded in the human resource frame, most closely resonate with my core beliefs, values, and assumptions, which guide and influence my practice.

The tenets that comprise the Human Resource frame highlight the importance of individual needs and motives. This frame operates on the assumptions that schools and classrooms, as other social systems, work best when needs are satisfied in a caring, trusting, work environment. Showing concern for others and providing ample opportunities for participation and shared decision making are among the ways to increase ownership and enlist commitment and involvement of the stakeholders (Bolman & Deal, 2002).

TRANSFORMATIONAL LEADERSHIP FRAMEWORK

Another Framework that has shaped my practice and integrates well with the Humanistic Resource Framework, are the principles embedded in the Transformational Leadership Framework. This framework, which links principles of adult learning theory (Anfara & Mertz, 2006) and transformational learning, suggests that significant learning in our lives involves meaning making that can lead to a transformation of our personality or worldview (Anfara & Mertz, 2006).

Since I was interested in exploring specifically the developmental process of principals who participated in sustained job-embedded learning over time, the developmental tenets of this theory strengthen the appropriateness of this theoretical framework, which have guided this project. Mezirow (in Anfara & Mertz, 2006),

INTRODUCTION

asserted that this type of learning is developmental, in that it involves "movement towards more developmentally progressive meaning perspectives."

METHODS

The author, vested in understanding the learning processes and individual experiences of school principals in a professional development setting, which could serve to build upon theory to challenge theoretical assumptions held prior to data gathering (Merriam, 1998), implemented an interpretive case study approach. Interpretive case study, a component of qualitative methodology, guided the further exploration of the problem centered on how principals construct meaning of their learning and change process, when they are provided with sustained job-embedded learning opportunities to learn with their peers.

The emphasis in this research was placed on learning what principals perceive happens when they engage in a professional learning community model over a sustained period of time, that closely embodies similar skill-sets, dispositions and attributes they are charged to implement and facilitate at their respective sites. Instrumental to the analyses and implications of this project are the types of data collected and analyzed.

- Summaries that synthesized the conversations and activities were completed after each Administrators' Professional Learning Community (PLC). These summaries facilitated the agenda of subsequent sessions with the principals.
- Complete descriptions of each of the PD modules provided to principals including the instructional materials that were used.
- In-depth individual interviews and focus groups with participant principals who received this professional development.
- District-wide achievement data.

JOURNEY

I vividly remember the trepidation and resistance that permeated the room when the phone rang early winter morning. Reluctantly, I answered the phone, anticipating the request from my colleague who directed a grant-funded university initiative. The request entailed the delivery of yet another well-intended, unaligned, and programmatic in-service on how to utilize data and increase data literacy to a rural school district.

As professors of a land-grant university, we both were members of an outreach effort that strived to build and sustain university-district partnerships with rural school districts throughout the state. Most of the schools in the state were identified as Schools in Need of Improvement (SINOI). Many of these rural school districts experienced continuous issues with access and funding, and were striving to comply with state mandates while grappling with the complex and elusive school improvement process.

INTRODUCTION

Prior to my current role as a professor whose work is centered on preparing prospective school leaders and providing comprehensive and continuous support to seated principals, I was a secondary principal of an urban school. Within this capacity, I was charged as the change agent of a school that was involved in the complex process of restructuring. This school had received a similar designation of SINOI, in the early years of the No Child Left Behind (NCLB) era. During this complex and pivotal time of facilitating my school through the deep school renewal journey, I was assigned two external facilitators by the state, to help assist with this initiative. One of the provisions of the Comprehensive School Reform Demonstration Act (CSRD) required the district and principal to attain the services of a state approved external facilitator. Another critical provision, required the principal with the assistance of the facilitator and the collaboration of the district, to identify a comprehensive school reform model, which would serve as one important catalyst to make the systemic changes required by the mandate.

The opportunity to select a reform model that most closely aligned with the complex needs of my school was one of the few areas where choice was involved. I capitalized on a small window of opportunity to incorporate my faculty in a shared-decision making process, which I used to leverage the change process. This was a critical opportunity to authentically incorporate and model effective leadership tenets embedded in the leadership literature. I engaged my faculty in a collective and comprehensive decision-making process which required my faculty to research many of the reform models available.

The faculty was charged with the task of working collaboratively in teams to use data and have purposeful conversations centered on determining which model would be the most appropriate and applicable for our school. The process, which led to the selection of the model, served to facilitate increased ownership, and commence the cultivation of a shared vision and collective purpose. This also served as a powerful means to apply the leadership tenets in applicable context. The culmination of this collective work effort resulted in the selection of the DuFour and Eaker Professional Learning Community Model as our guide.

A significant portion of my Comprehensive School Reform Demonstration funds were allocated for sending teams of faculty to Lincolnshire, Illinois. I also accompanied my team members and the external facilitator to Lincolnshire. In an effort to help ensure school-wide implementation, funds were utilized for sending team members from Lincolnshire to reach my entire faculty and leadership team.

This paramount experience in my career afforded me with first-hand knowledge and insight to the intricacies of the complex, yet attainable change process. The acquisition and application of this learning served to challenge certain assumptions, while solidifying others. My school became the platform in which I implemented and integrated the underpinnings of theoretical frameworks, models, and school initiatives. Since my overarching charge entailed providing evidence of progress, it was necessary that I examined both the strengths and limitations of theories and models. From this vantage point, I gleaned invaluable insight when applying theories

INTRODUCTION

and models in context to affecting significant change in the midst of the current school culture, which embodied deeply held beliefs and practices. Not uncommon, most of the stakeholders in the school did not or were not ready to embrace the externally imposed change initiatives.

This comprehensive experience has been an insurmountable force which continues to shape and define my philosophical underpinnings comprising my conceptual framework. This well-defined yet evolving framework is embedded with core beliefs, leadership principles acquired from experts in the field, in addition to my own insights gleaned from working to build individual, collective and organizational leadership capacity. This framework work guides both the purpose of my practice and the philosophy of my practice, which has been reflected in this project.

STAYING THE COURSE

The guiding principles of the university outreach effort aligned with my core values and beliefs, centered on my deep-seated commitment to build leadership capacity in rural schools, where access to universities and quality professional development frequently served as a barrier. However, the learning that has shaped my belief in and commitment to systemic change processes in light of the complexity, served to facilitate the increased dissonance I experienced in participating in superficial professional development efforts that were frustrating for the recipient school districts as well as myself. These well intended, yet frequently haphazardly delivered efforts, served to perpetuate the historical role of providing professional development to districts, which has become increasingly incongruent in meeting the challenges of the districts and changing roles of the principals.

Pervaded with the feeling of discord and disagreement on the purpose and delivery of professional development, I obliged my colleague's request to conduct the site visit that morning. Upon arrival at the high-school, the demeanor of the high school faculty who were in attendance at this in-service was indicative of how they would likely receive this training late in the afternoon. The coaches sat slouched in the back of the room, wearing the all too familiar "this too, shall pass look," in their eyes.

The resonation with the faculty's disconnect, prompted a different approach to this training. After providing the faculty with an overview of the session, centered on strategies to effectively use data to inform instruction and decision making, I became more interested in collecting data which reflected their perspective, individual and collective assessments on where they were and what they felt was needed. I was interested in learning how much experience they have had in utilizing data, how they made decisions, and what their learning outcomes were. This approach, served to engage the faculty, as we began to actively co-construct this meeting, and prospective meetings which followed at this school.

INTRODUCTION

TURNING-POINT

While there were many disjointed pieces involved in the delivery of professional development provided by the university, there was a poignant strength, which was eventually utilized as a turning point in enhancing the university-district partnership. The team of coaches and facilitators kept coming back! The central office leaders continued to demonstrate receptivity to the emerging partnership, in light of the existing discrepancies.

After making an initial connection with the teachers and principal at this high school within this district, I felt that I had something I might be able to build-upon, and an emerging idea that I wanted to explore. While the relationship with the school district was still tenuous and evolving, I felt that there was a sense of readiness on the part of the faculty, the principal, as well as central office; contingent that the collaboration and services were perceived as relevant and purposeful.

I asked my colleague who directed the outreach initiative to focus my efforts with this one school and district. She obliged my request. After several weeks of returning to the school, as part of the team of facilitators and coaches, I began to build a relationship and trust with central office. During this critical time, the district was also working to strengthen structures and put new structures into place, which reflected more closely the voices of the teachers as well as adhering to state mandated initiatives. The district responded to the voices of the teachers by bringing back a common planning period. Training for walk-throughs and the formal implementation of Professional Learning Communities were among these initiatives.

At that point in time, the focus of professional development efforts was placed on district-wide training and development of the teachers. The principals were perceived as Instructional Leaders charged with the implementation and oversight of the initiatives put in place. The following quote from one of the participants supports this perception.

> Principals as "Instructional Leaders" have to support the PD and be active participants along with their staff in order for this to work." As Instructional Leaders, we have to be role models and learn along with them.

In light of the district-wide Professional Development efforts supported by the district, the PD continued to have minimal impact on building teacher capacity and increasing district-wide student-achievement. While the principals were included in these trainings, the principals whom were charged with the oversight of district-wide initiatives did not have the capacity to support implementation processes in the classrooms and provide differentiated instructional support to their teachers. In addition, most of these principals did not participate in Educational Leadership Programs that provided a focus on instructional leadership and on leading change initiatives that required a deep understanding of systemic change processes.

INTRODUCTION

EMERGING PARTNERSHIP

Initially, the services provided by the university were in the form of technical support intended to build capacity of teachers and principals in using data to inform instructional practice. As the partnership evolved and the vision to change the existing culture to a collegial culture (Sergiovanni, 2009) by changing system-wide practices solidified, the need to build principal leadership capacity became our immediate priority. It was agreed upon that the structures and interventions that were put into place would have limited efficacy and hold little promise for sustainability, if the principals did not buy-in to the change, have the instructional skills and capacity to guide teachers' development, or were able to maximize the use of interventions and structures that the district provided (Ludeke, 2011).

ADMINISTRATORS' PROFESSIONAL LEARNING COMMUNITY

Having had first-hand experience with the implementation process of the DuFour and Eaker Professional Learning Community Model (1998), several underlying presumptions guided my research inquiry. First, I believed that this and similar models can be effective in facilitating deep cultural change if the correct conditions were present. Second, I did not feel that the principals, who were charged with guiding their teachers through the implementation of this model, understood the underlying philosophy of this model and the complex elements entailed in this model. Nor did they exhibit the beliefs, behaviors, and skill-sets required to guide and support their teachers through this process. Additionally, I did not feel that they understood that this model serves as a catalyst for facilitating deep change that can transform the norms of the school culture (DuFour, DuFour, & Eaker, 2008).

I did not believe that the principals knew how to help their teachers make important connections between this model, their practice, and student achievement. I also did not feel that the principals held the individual and collective skill sets to have purposeful conversations with their teachers about improving their practice and the fundamental role of PLCs (Ludeke, 2011). I was eager to further explore the postulation that principals may not be able to implement and facilitate a high functioning PLC as described by the literature, without the principals engaging in a deep learning process that would help them to acquire the skill sets, behaviors, and dispositions necessary for implementing the level of change that was expected from them.

I felt the urgency to further understand the processes involved and how the principals made meaning of sustained professional development, where the focus was placed on building leadership capacity. I wanted to build-upon the scant research that presents a paradigm-shift from expending the focus on teacher professional development to principal professional development to address the current problem. Building upon an emergent theory, through the implementation of an interpretative case study approach held the possibility of influencing policy, practice, and future research (Merriam, 1998).

INTRODUCTION

Research (Evans, 1996 and Fullan, 2001, 2008) has suggested the need for systemic and fundamental change in how schools are organized and the kind of principal leadership needed to bring about fundamental change. In light of these findings, significant gaps exist between the current expectations that are at the center of the changing role of leadership, and the level of professional development provided to principals. The project strived to further explore this problem. Principals seated prior to the paradigm shift that has markedly changed the role of the principalship, are charged with changing the culture of their schools and guiding reform efforts that provide evidence of transforming cultures that can produce high levels of student-achievement. However, many of these principals have never engaged in this deep change process, requiring principals to create and sustain cultures of collaboration for the purpose of increasing student achievement. The findings of this project have potential implications for informing university-district partnerships, principal preparation programs, the hiring practices of the institutions, the design and delivery of professional development, and further research. With the unwavering support of the Associate Superintendent and Central Office Administration, the formation of an Administrators' Professional Community was created.

ORGANIZATION OF THE BOOK

Extensive multifaceted data were collected and analyzed throughout this project, in an effort to capture the voices and learning of the principals and participants throughout the 5-year partnership. Principle to this project is that the voices of the participants and emergent themes throughout the journey of the partnership are captured and brought to light. The voices of all participants have been embedded into context throughout the chapters of this book. In an effort to maintain confidentiality of the participants, fictitious names are utilized.

CHAPTER 1: THE EVOLVING ROLE OF THE PRINCIPAL

The stage for this chapter was set by providing a chronological progression of the historical events which continue to impact the role of the principal. As the role of the principal has changed from manager to the role of instructional leader in an era of continuous reform efforts, there is increasing pressure for accountability and for leading innovation. By providing this contextual landscape, this chapter strives to introduce the problem of school leaders' inability to effectively lead instructional change efforts in their schools, which frequently require the principal to facilitate deep cultural shifts within the school.

CHAPTER 2: UNIVERSITY-DISTRICT PARTNERSHIPS

This chapter expanded on the idea of university and school-district partnerships as potentially being well situated to increase the learning, teaching, and leadership

INTRODUCTION

capacity of all levels of the educational system. Principals are currently expected to facilitate comprehensive school improvement efforts, frequently implementing the model of teacher professional learning communities to increase student achievement and meet the needs of diverse learners. However, many of these principals do not have experience in working with cultures of collaboration for the purpose of increasing student achievement.

Chapter 2 sets the stage for the need of principals' development and levels of support to align to the systemic innovations they are leading. This chapter highlighted the changing role of university-district partnerships, as they worked together to address existing gaps and opportunities for attaining mutually agreed upon outcomes. Also, discussed, were the challenges and barriers presented when interdependent relationships were commenced between two institutions characterized by differing cultures, expectations, and capacities. The conditions required to sustain the partnership in light of the differences and complex relationship, were introduced.

CHAPTER 3: DEVELOPING THE MODEL FOR THE ADMINISTRATORS' PLC

As PLCs increasingly attain widespread acceptance as a school reform initiative, there is little research that sheds light on the voices of principals who understand that PLCs are an increasingly accepted approach of facilitating deep cultural and systemic change within the school organization. The author operated on the premise that there are few principals who have participated in PLCs as teachers, and even fewer principals who have participated in the change process evoked in participating in a Principals' PLC. The work that emerged as the result of the partnership between two institutions provided the prospect to further the research through the implementation of an interpretive case study approach.

This chapter provided the process of the formation and continuous development of the university-district partnership that facilitated the conceptualization of the Administrators' Professional Learning Community. As the Administrators' PLC developed and progressed throughout the 5-year partnership, a variety of resources were utilized and developed. The resources and methods utilized were comprehensively addressed in this chapter.

CHAPTER 4: INSIGHTS ON THE PRINCIPALS PRIOR TO THE PLC

This chapter formally introduced the principals and administrators who participated in this project. The focus of this chapter and the forthcoming chapters centered on findings and implications are placed on further understanding how these principals made contextual meaning of their learning throughout the process of their sustained professional development. These findings strived to fully describe the sequences (Rowlands, 2005) of the principals' individual and collective learning, which have bearing on the conditions that determine innovation processes and theory building (Rowlands, 2005). Analyses from the emergent themes were provided,

INTRODUCTION

which had significant implications for guiding the early and continual efforts of the Administrators' PLC. Finally, within the context of specific themes, the author shared the process of how the collective learning as a group guided the practice and continuous development of the Administrators' PLC.

CHAPTER 5: CHANGED PRINCIPAL PERCEPTIONS

The focus of this chapter was centered on understanding how the principals perceived the relevance and applicability of the Administrators' PLC. The author commenced this chapter with highlighting the initial principal perceptions and understanding of the purpose and significance of engaging in sustained professional development as a district-wide effort. The findings centered on the principals' individual and collective changed perceptions after participating in the Administrators' PLC for two years was shared. Chapter 5 concluded with a discussion highlighting centralized instructional practices within the district, evidenced by the districts' increased capacity to proactively respond to and implement externally mandated state and federal initiatives.

CHAPTER 6: LINKING CHANGED PRINCIPAL PERCEPTIONS TO PRACTICE

Central to the theme in Chapter 5, was to convey the ideas and beliefs of principals' initial thoughts pertaining to the relevance of their participation in professional development delivered through the formation of the Administrators' PLC. Findings of principals changed perceptions were embedded into the chapter. The chapter was concluded with a discussion which highlighted the implications that changed principal perceptions had for both the principal participants and central office.

Chapter 6 paid special attention to understanding the connection between changed principal perceptions, principal behaviors, and priorities. The bearing these changes had on their practice as a principal were brought to light through the participants' voices. Several themes emerged that provided indication of how principal participants' thinking of what it now means to be a principal has changed.

CHAPTER 7: PRINCIPALS' PERCEPTIONS CENTERED ON THE UNIVERSITY-DISTRICT PARTNERSHIP

Chapter 7 explored the perceptions of the principal participants, as it concerned the sustained effort of the university-district partnership. In this chapter, the principals shared their insights concerning their involvement with the university, which endeavored to build leadership capacity through the development and implementation of the Administrators' PLC. The principals shared their individual and collective insights pertaining to the outcomes of their individual and collective experiences.

The participants provided insights on the conditions necessary for sustaining the partnership, addressed barriers, and provided recommendations for facilitating

INTRODUCTION

continuous improvement efforts. The findings from the emergent themes have implications centered on issues of continuous improvement, replication, and sustainability. The inferences of these findings were expected to promote the advancement of research in an area that warrants further inquiry.

CHAPTER 8: CONCLUSION

The final chapter strived to synthesize the findings as it connected to further understanding of the problem, which compelled the author to write this book. This chapter embedded the author's narrative, which brought to light the researcher's voice. This narrative provided the reader with insights on the researcher, portraying her theoretical frameworks, experiences, and assumptions, as they have played an instrumental role in momentum to partake in the university-district partnership.

Within the context of the analyses, specific implications were brought to light. These implications facilitated deep discussions which led to specific recommendations as they aligned to the implications derived from the analyses. The final chapter concluded with the author's reflection and a closing passage.

CHAPTER 1

THE EVOLVING ROLE OF THE PRINCIPAL

CONTEXTUAL LANDSCAPE

In a post No Child Left Behind (NCLB) era, buzzing conversations between teachers and administrators preoccupied and overwhelmed with school change efforts has become common practice. With several decades spanning school reform efforts that continue to pervade our schools, whole-school reform (McDougall, Saunders, & Goldenberg, 2007) has increasingly become the cultural norm. Conversations and reactions regarding the newest reform initiative and the effects of these reforms have become the center of concern both in and out of our school buildings. The influence and weight of perpetual reform has been incorporated into the school climate. Due to comprehensive attempts to change and improve our schools, in many cases, the promising reform efforts and initiatives continue to fall short.

NEW ROLE CONCEPTUALIZATIONS OF THE PRINCIPALSHIP IN AN ERA OF ACCOUNTABILITY

> Before, you ran your school, you carried your budget, you hardly ever saw anyone. Now, suddenly it's different thinking, a different conversation. We are all learners. We are all to be involved in learning. It is not just about being an administrator, it's about being instructional leaders.
> -A Veteran New York City Principal–Wallace Foundation

The unwavering culture of comprehensive reform over the past decades has irrevocably changed how the role of the principal is now conceptualized. The political hold (Hess & Petrilli, 2006) of forthcoming reforms, or the shape that future reforms may take, is changeable and uncertain. Notwithstanding the uncertainty, or the position one takes regarding the era of accountability, educational leadership literature and policy, have both served to change how we conceptualize the role of the principal.

What have become more certain are the concepts that have emerged from this era, which serve to inform our conceptions and expectations of the principal's role. Theories and models of collaboration, capacity building, instructional leader, systems thinking, transformative leadership, student-centered learning, continuous learning, data-informed decision making, and a community of learners, are examples of some of the interchangeably used concepts which have taken hold within the context of the pK-20 education pipeline. These theoretical frameworks and models

CHAPTER 1

are increasingly used to define the conceptions and expectations we have for the 21st century principal.

THE PREMISE OF THE 5-YEAR UNIVERSITY-DISTRICT PROJECT

The indelibility of this conceptual change has implications for how the pK20 educational system responds to the challenges and opportunities presented. As principals make the transition from manager to instructional leader, they are required to lead instructional change efforts in their schools, which frequently involve the principal's ability to build leadership capacity among colleagues (Lambert, 1998). This chapter introduced the problem of school leaders' inability to effectively lead instructional change efforts in their schools. These efforts frequently require the principal to implement the concepts that have become associated with the evolving role of the principal. This book is centered on the following assertions, which have been explored through the implementation of the 5-year project.

- I have made the assertion that many new and seated principals, who are currently charged with the responsibility of implementing systems-based models that could potentially serve as catalysts for transforming the existing school culture, may not currently have the ability to facilitate comprehensive models of change without having experienced the change process and without having provided evidence of their own professional growth.
- Another premise that has been explored in the 5-year project that facilitated this book is the proposal of a systemic pK-20 pipeline approach that provides continuous opportunities for building and supporting leadership capacity in adherence to the tenets of how the role of the principalship is now defined.
- These efforts must be directed toward seated principals and school administrators who are responsible for leading school-wide change efforts for the purpose of changing conditions that can hold promise for meeting the diverse needs of students in the 21st century.

Chapter 1 provides the reader with an overview of NCLB. I have expounded on the concepts that embody the evolving conceptualization of the principal, which have been informed in large part by the implemented policy and literature that has been published during this era of accountability. An account of how professional development is changing to more closely meet the demands society has for the principal of the 21st century is provided.

Chapter 1 concludes with a brief discussion on the disconnected practices that exist within the current system of educational leadership. The existing gaps within the pK-20 system facilitated the opportunity to direct our professional development efforts toward the practicing or seated principals within the district, for the intent of building leadership capacity to effectively lead the reform models they have been charged to implement. The development of the practice to place an increased emphasis on principal development; the concept to provide the principal participants

14

and university-district participants the opportunity to engage in a sustained learning community where all stakeholders shared practice; the emergent role of the partnership; the findings of the project, and the implications of the findings will be explored in depth in subsequent chapters.

THE NO CHILD LEFT BEHIND ACT IN AN ERA OF ACCOUNTABILITY

The No Child Left Behind Act of 2001 aimed to determine students' annual academic progress (AYP) (Haretos, 2005) does not denote the beginning of a long school reform era. NCLB, does however, signify probably the most ambitious school improvement policy enacted, which attempts to hold the educational community accountable for increasing student achievement for *all* students. Hess and Petrilli (2006) underscore that NCLB brought far-reaching and all-encompassing changes to the 37-year-old Elementary and Secondary Education Act (ESEA) which preceded NCLB. The NCLB law, intended to put America's schools on a "new path of reform," and on a "new path of results" (Office of the White Press Secretary, 2002 in Hess & Petrilli, 2006), "thrust the nation's educators, schools, and school districts in a new world of federal educational accountability" (Hess & Petrilli (2006). The enactment of this law and the embedded politics, has fostered a culture of controversy, skepticism, and many promising approaches to whole-school reform that have fallen short of their assurance to produce substantial changes in teaching and learning (McDougall et al. 2007). Whole-school reform models have been reproached in their attempt to facilitate school change, as often the changes fail to make much difference in the intellectual lives of teachers and their students (Goodman, 1995).

Whether the politics of NCLB will hold is uncertain (Hess & Petrilli, 2006). However, concepts centered on the potential impact of conceptions that have implications for schools are likely to remain. Concepts such as moving from a culture of isolation to a culture of interdependence and collaboration; the belief that *all* students can learn and should learn, as this is the moral imperative (Fullan, 2001, 2005); student-centered learning; professional development for teachers and leaders that embody learning-centered principles and shared practice, giving way to the "drive-by professional development (Wiburg & Brown, 2007); cultivating a collegial school (Sergiovanni, 2007); second-order change principles (Fullan; Senge; Evans, 1996, 2001 as well as other researchers; and redefining the parameters and boundaries of partnerships, exemplify the impact on the principal's role. These theories, which have led to the development of conceptual frameworks, models, and the passage of additional initiatives and standards are likely to remain. These significant changes present considerable challenges to an educational system that was not designed to incorporate these conceptualizations.

On the other side of the argument, this reformation summons new opportunities for reconceptualization as the expectation to practice differently and meet the needs of diverse students in a global economy is gaining wide-spread attention and increased acceptance. Our current challenge is centered on the ability of the system to increase the connections between the standards and prevailing structures which correspond to the changing role and expectations of the principal.

HISTORICAL ROLE OF THE PRINCIPAL

Prior to the NCLB era, the definition of what it meant to be an effective principal has changed from management to instructional leadership. Matthews and Crow (2010) mention that the early responsibilities of principals had little to do with leadership and more to do with unlocking the doors and managing the daily routines. The underlying implications of the shift from management to principal as learner (Matthews & Crow, 2010) are numerous and complex for all stakeholders. The Federal No Child Left Behind law and state-level accountability mandates have placed principals on the front lines in the struggle to ensure that every child succeeds as a learner (Wallace Foundation, 2006). It can be inferred that principals who operate under these mandates, who perform their job as a competent manager, increases the probability of losing their jobs (Wallace Foundation, 2006).

PRINCIPAL AS MANAGER

Historically, the role of the principalship was defined much differently than it is in a post NCLB era. Successful schools in the mid-20th century served a fundamentally different purpose than the schools of the 21st century (Hargreaves & Fink, 2003. The principals in that era were not perceived as "change agents," and "instructional leaders" who were charged with building teacher capacity to help teachers implement student-centered practices with the prospect of yielding high levels of student achievement. This daunting expectation that we now have placed on our principals in a historically short-time period simply ceased to exist.

Portin, Alegano, Knapp, and Marzolf (2006) eloquently described a successful principal in that era as one who ran clean and regimented institutions that closely resembled a "well-oiled machine." The principal was not expected to embrace the elements required of an instructional leader or to have the skills of transformational leadership that can facilitate deep cultural shifts within the organizational school culture. Rather, this type of principal was considered successful if he could maintain the "status quo" and perpetuate the norms and traditions that have been in existence for generations.

Behind excellent teaching and excellent schools is excellent leadership
—Wallace Foundation, 2006

PRINCIPAL AS INSTRUCTIONAL LEADER

The elements correlated with the principal's performance in an era of accountability, look very different than they did in the mid-20th century. Today's principals are expected to serve as "engaged instructional leaders" (Wallace Foundation, 2006) who can develop effective teams in their schools to drive sustained improvements in teaching and learning in every classroom. In addition to these core elements that redefine the role of principal as effective manager, the principal as instructional leader is expected to provide a range of support to teachers, create a supportive team culture at their school in which all adults share successes and challenges in a sympathetic but rigorous way, being mindful to both effective classroom practices as well as ineffective ones (Wallace Foundation, 2006). Further, these principals also are expected to have the courage to challenge accustomed practices, if deemed ineffective. This can be interpreted as challenging the assumptions of the "status-quo," which have permeated the long-standing culture of the complex organizational system of the school (Fullan, 2001).

> Leadership is second only to classroom instruction among all school-related factors that contribute to what students learn at school.
> —Wallace Foundation, 2006

INSTRUCTIONAL LEADERSHIP: SECOND TO TEACHING

From a historical perspective, the growing body of research that makes a case for correlating effective school leaders to increased student achievement is still a young concept. Rooted in these findings is the assertion that school leadership is second to teaching for affecting student-achievement. Matthews and Crow (2010; Hargreaves and Fink (2003); Sergiovanni (2006) and Lynch (2012) are several of many researchers who assert that the principal's role as instructional leader is central to impacting student achievement. These researchers conclude that independent of the teacher, the principal exists as the most powerful influence affecting academic performance. Lynch (2012) expounds upon the magnified role of the principal as instructional leader by highlighting five responsibilities associated with this role.

DiPaola and Walther-Thomas (2003 in Lynch, 2012) correlated the first task of the principal as instructional leader to be centered on defining and communicating the school's educational mission. Effective instructional leaders emphasize the importance of educating all students, to include students with identified disabilities. Second, effective instructional leaders provide evidence of supporting teacher use of research-based practices. The third supposition involves the ability of the instructional leader to supervise teaching and substantiate the school's commitment to teachers. The research underscores that this behavior leads to increasing the level of a teacher's sense of commitment, belonging, and self-worth. The fourth identified factor requires the instructional leader to monitor student progress, correlated with enhancing students' self-worth which could promote higher academic performance. The fifth attribute that encompasses the effectiveness of an instructional leader is the ability to establish and maintain the same high expectations for all students.

CHAPTER 1

CAUSE AND EFFECT OF NEW UNDERSTANDING

Drawing from the stream of research, there is considerable support for the premise that the role of instructional leadership is second to impacting student learning. This emergent view and increasing acceptance poses significant challenges, as the system of educational leadership at many levels is disconnected (Wallace Foundation, 2006) and does not currently support this understanding.

DISCONNECTED PRACTICES THROUGHOUT THE PK-20 PIPELINE

The elements that are needed for developing, supporting, and sustaining instructional leaders are frequently not present, are fragmented, or are observed at various developmental stages throughout the pK-20 continuum. A study conducted by the Wallace Foundation (2006) suggests that the definition of what constitutes a "successful leader' is poorly understood and defined and is not yet well-enough connected to the goal of promoting learning. The study indicated that while the standards focused on the knowledge and skills today's leaders need, much less emphasis is placed on the specific behaviors that are likely to promote better teaching and learning in schools.

The Wallace Foundation study, in addition to similar studies that have been conducted foster a sense of urgency to examine more closely the structures and practices that can promote the development of leadership behaviors. The standards that have been adopted (SREB, 2008, 2012; Wallace Foundation, 2006) in the era of accountability need to be more closely connected to structures which include continuous professional development, university-preparation programs, and district hiring practices. While I have addressed these topics in subsequent chapters in context to the university-district project, the remainder of this chapter provides an overview of professional development, the elements embedded in professional learning communities and whole-school reform models, as they are interrelated to the changing role of the principal.

HISTORICAL FUNCTION OF PROFESSIONAL DEVELOPMENT

One of the confounding educational dilemmas confronting school leaders today is that in spite of years of educational reforms, students have not attained the level of proficiency in core academic subjects necessary to compete in a global economy (SREB, 2012). Historically, educational reform efforts have focused on teacher professional development. More recently, the focus has been placed on providing job-embedded teacher development as it connects to changing teacher behaviors that can have an impact on improving student learning outcomes (Richmond & Manokore, 2010). Paradoxically, in an era marked by continuous improvement and reform, much less attention has been directed toward the sustained professional development of school leaders, who are charged with facilitating organizational change for cultivating conditions that improve student learning (Evans, 2001; Fullan, 2005).

COLLABORATIVE PROFESSIONAL DEVELOPMENT TO FACILITATE CHANGE

The limited success of school reform efforts over the last 40 years, has served as a catalyst for researchers to examine how change may be achieved in schools for the purpose of improving teaching practices and increasing student achievement (Waldron & McLeskey, 2010). These findings have served to influence the progression of professional development and the changing expectations the educational community places on the outcomes of professional development. Waldron and McLeskey (2010) posit a key finding that was prevalent in their research which linked collaboration of professionals in a school setting as an integral component to the school change process. Research conducted during the era of accountability and after the passage of NCLB in 2001, specifically links the complex collaborative process to school change.

RECULTURING PROCESS

The concept and need for reculturing a school is interdependent on the collaboration process, which determines the extent of whether the efforts of collaboration will yield the outcome of improved instructional practices and student-achievement. Reculturing a school involves the examination of (DuFour, Eaker, & Burnette (2002); Fullan, 2005) beliefs, expectations, and assumptions, for the purpose of school change that can facilitate a collective sense of purpose (DuFour, Eaker, & Burnette, (2002); DuFour, DuFour, Eaker, & Karhnek, 2010). The outcome of improving instructional practices conducive to increasing student achievement is not likely to occur without engaging in a complex collaborative process that can lead to the acquisition of new values, beliefs, and norms. Eaker, DuFour, and Burnette (2002) make the case that professional learning communities are the best hope for reculturing a school. They assert that if the school community is intent about changing and improving the climates and outcomes of schooling, features of the existing school culture need to be examined and changed.

The increased acceptance for collaboration and reculturing to occur in our schools, informed by the educational leadership literature, has contributed to the increased implementation of professional learning communities in pK-12 schools nationwide and internationally. The concept of collaborative learning and professional learning communities precedes the widely accepted Professional Learning Communities model developed. (Eaker, DuFour, & Burnette, 2002). The approach of bringing professionals together to build professional capacity, change the school culture, and provide a platform for continuous professional development is gaining increased precedence throughout the pK-12 educational system. This paradigm shift in the role of professional development has profound implications for the changing role of the principal. The school principal, who is increasingly expected to perform as the instructional leader as well as manager, is also charged with leading these professional learning communities in their schools.

ELEMENTS OF EFFECTIVE LEADERSHIP PRACTICES

Wong and Nicotera (2007) describe the elements of leadership practices that correlate to school-improvement needs in an era of educational-accountability reform. Their findings reinforce the discoveries of many prominent researchers during this era. The findings concluded that principals of productive schools focused on issues central to bringing about improvements in instructional practices and student learning. The critical elements centered on the principal's ability to build capacity by developing teachers' knowledge and skills, strengthening the school's connection with parents and the community, and the ability to promote a school wide professional community that facilitates reflective dialogue and collaboration on instructional practices.

PROFESSIONAL LEARNING COMMUNITIES

Research conducted by the Ontario's Principal Council (2009) posits that professional learning communities are an instrument for the enhancement of learning, teaching, and leadership capacity at all levels of the educational system. This assertion has implications for higher education institutions and university-district partnerships, which will be expounded on in Chapter 2. The Ontario Principal Council point out that the study of PLCs has been studied and led by prominent educational researchers who make a persuasive case for the implementation of PLCs as a significant means of building teacher, school leader, and system capacity. Many of these educational leaders who comprise the school improvement research community include researchers such as: Peter Senge, Richard Stiggins, Louise Stoll, Richard DuFour, Rebecca DuFour, Robert Eaker, Michael Fullan, Andy Hargreaves, and Larry Lazotte (Ontario Principals' Council, 2009).

In light of the compelling rationale for implementing professional learning communities, additional research and development is still needed. Matthews and Crow (2010) assert that although there has not been a lot of research on PLCs, some researchers have found positive effects on students' success in schools where the critical elements of a PLC were found. The author provides a conceptual framework of a PLC and highlight the elements most commonly found in what the research defines as effective PLCs. Some of the elements described are also likely to be found in other whole-school reform models that intend to have an impact on affecting deep change within and across the system.

> A PLC is composed of collaborative teams whose members work interdependently to achieve common goals for which members are mutually accountable.
>
> DuFour, DuFour, Eaker, and Many (2010)

OPERATIONAL DEFINITION OF A PLC

While there may be some variation in how a PLC is defined, the educational literature describes a professional learning community as: a school environment where teachers work collaboratively to improve student achievement within a structure of support provided by the school administrator (Ontario Principals' Council, 2009). In these schools, principals create a culture where teachers work actively in teams with the shared purpose of producing successful learning outcomes for all students. Eaker et al., (2002) expound on the critical component of a collaborative culture, which must be embedded into a professional learning community. Eaker, DuFour, and Burnette (2002) stress that every major decision related to the learning mission must be made through collaborative processes. Fundamental assumptions that have been made are:

- If schools are to improve, staff must develop the capacity to function as professional learning communities.
- If schools are to function as professional learning communities, they must develop a collaborative culture.
- If schools are to overcome their tradition of teacher isolation, teachers must learn to work in effective, high-performing teams.

Eaker, DuFour, and Burnette (2002) assert that special attention must be paid to the "interdependence" and "common goals" if we are going to have high-quality collaboration and truly effective teams.

> Change is technically simple and socially complex
> Michal Fullan, 2005

The paradigm shift required for these conditions to be met, often requiring that the school moves from a culture of deep ingrained isolated practices to a culture of collaboration which requires shared-practice, transparency, trust, a collective sense of purpose, and a team of professionals who value continuous learning, can be daunting for the school principal. Our experiences in the partnership, which will be addressed in forthcoming chapters, is that many well-intended and diligent school leaders underestimate the extent of the changes that are intended. Further, the organizational capacity has existing gaps that serve as barriers for implementing and sustaining complex reform efforts without sustained external supports. The issue of under capacity at all levels present throughout the pK-20 system is one of the assumptions made by the author which is discussed throughout the book.

CAPACITY TO IMPLEMENT SYSTEMIC CHANGE INITIATIVES

I argue the case that many practicing principals today, charged with leading professional learning communities, regardless of the model implemented, underestimate the complexity and lack an understanding of the complex change process embedded in the principles of change theory addressed in the educational literature. Glickman et al. (2010) suggest that many schools lack the capacity to launch significant improvement efforts with a reasonable chance of success. Glickman et al. (2010) attribute poor communication, low trust levels, and the absence of collaboration, indicative of the school's culture serve as potential barriers for increasing readiness to engage in an effective change process.

PLCS AND THE INSTRUCTIONAL LEADER

The author makes the assumption that many well-intended practicing principals do not have a full understanding of the many complex elements that are found in most successful PLCs. I assert that many principals do not initially correlate the implementation of a PLC with significant change efforts, as many principals equate a PLC as a program or a programmatic initiative, rather than a reform initiative intended to reframe and redefine the system. Matthews and Crow (2010) suggest that while PLCs are not to be perceived as a "panacea for solving all of the problems in a school," the PLC process can provide options and opportunities for growth and learning with colleagues in a way that previous reform initiatives have not been able to provide.

ELEMENTS EMBEDDED IN A PROFESSIONAL LEARNING COMMUNITY

Matthews, Williams, and Stewart (2007) in Matthews and Crow (2010) contributed to the PLC literature through the development of ten cultural elements that are found in most effective PLCs.

Principal Leadership That Is Focused On Student Learning. This element speaks directly to the changed conceptual role of the principal, which has been interwoven in this chapter. Our expectations of the principal have changed from principal as an efficient manager to a principal who can develop the necessary conditions to help adults in the school continually improve their ability to ensure students gain the knowledge and skills that are essential to the success of students in the 21st century. The underlying implication is that the school principal is now adept with adult learning principles, and has the skills in the area of clinical supervision, which comprises a critical component of the role of the instructional leader. Glickman et al. (2010) use the metaphor of supervisory glue to link the role and purpose of supervision with an effective school; "We can think of supervision as the glue of a successful school."

COMMON MISSION, VISION, VALUES, AND GOALS THAT ARE FOCUSED ON TEACHING AND LEARNING

As defined in this context by Matthews and Crow (2003) in Matthews and Crow (2010), a mission provides the foundation for creating a vision through the process of defining the school's core values and creating goals in accomplishing the vision. DuFour, DuFour, Eaker, and Karhanek, (2010) assert that the mission serves to clarify the purpose, which can help establish priorities, asking the question, "Why do we exist?"

Participative leadership that focuses on teaching and learning. Shared leadership practices are a requisite condition in an effective professional learning community. In a PLC, principals must share leadership with other stakeholders in the school (Matthews & Crow, 2010). The practice of shared leadership has been described in a variety of terms. Democratic leadership, distributed leadership, collective leadership, and school leadership are terms that describe the process of involving stakeholders, specifically teachers, in the collective decision-making process within the school (Matthews & Crow, 2010).

High-Trust embedded in school culture. The quality and attribute of "trust," cannot be over-emphasized as paramount in any school improvement effort. Sergiovanni (2010) refers to trust as one of the moral principles to which the school is committed.

Interdependent culture that sustains continuous improvement in teaching and learning. Many of the aforementioned researchers, who have contributed to the work of PLCs, address the role that interdependency plays in developing and sustaining effective PLCs. Within the context of a PLC, teachers learn how to share classroom practices with other teachers which can facilitate a community of learners.

Teaming that is collaborative. Creating the structure of collaborative teams where teachers build capacity to learn interdependently is paramount in a PLC. The literature on PLCs asserts that it is improbable to have a PLC without collaborative teams.

Decision making based on data and research. Another critical element which requires time and effort to develop is the understanding of the role of data, and the ability to apply and act upon the data to inform decisions. From the perspective of the partnership stakeholders, this area can require much professional development and opportunities for practice, for both teachers and principals. Matthews and Crow (2010) and Holcomb (2004) as well as many other researchers who have contributed to the educational leadership literature, agree that using research and data-based decision making is essential in facilitating collaboration, providing participative leadership, and guiding instructional decisions.

Use of continuous assessment to improve learning. The use of continuous assessment consists of a continuous cycle of examining and acting on the results from student data that drives continuous learning. The use of formative assessment (Moss & Brookhart, 2009) is one type of assessment that can improve student achievement and raise teacher quality when implemented effectively.

Academic success for all students with systems of prevention and intervention. In effective PLCs, principals and teachers work together to examine existing structures and processes for providing strategies for prevention and intervention of students who are behind or are at risk of failure. The interventions embedded in the method of Response to Intervention (RtI), which focuses on how students respond to systematic and increasingly more intensive levels of instructional interventions (McLaughlin, 2009), has implications for examining system-wide processes within the school.

CHAPTER 1

Professional development that is teacher driven and embedded in daily work. Research to support "job embedded" professional development (Matthews & Crow, 2010) is replacing the "drive-by" professional development that was often the norm for delivering professional development to teachers and principals for many years.

THEMES OF CAPACITY BUILDING AND COLLABORATION

This chapter highlighted the external forces that have served to permanently change the contextual landscape for principals. The systemic changes which have occurred in an era of accountability have a profound impact on the educational pipeline which consists of pK-12 school districts who hire teachers and principals, and post-secondary institutions whose efforts are centered on teacher and leadership preparation. Two reoccurring themes that have become prevalent in this context are the concepts of *capacity building* and *collaboration*. The effect of implementing the complex tenets entailed in these concepts which are found in conceptual frameworks, models, as well as state and national mandates, are felt across the pK-20 system. Universities and school districts are increasingly challenged to re-examine existing structures and practices to include hiring, delivery of professional development, leadership preparation, as well as how universities and districts partner together to achieve specific outcomes. As these separate yet interdependent systems strive to build the individual and collective capacity of teachers and leaders who are better prepared to meet the daunting tasks of educating and leading in the 21st century, these systems are presented with opportunities to address existing systemic gaps, build internal capacities within and across systems, and redefine the context of their collaborative partnerships.

CONCLUSION

The purpose of this chapter was to provide the reader with an overview of the external change forces that have indelibly changed how the role of the principal is perceived, placing new and complex demands on the principal. A review of the literature centered on the change process, and the elements incorporated in the conceptual frameworks and models were embedded in the chapter. I have introduced the problem of school leaders' inability to effectively lead instructional change efforts in their schools which frequently require the principals to implement concepts that have become associated with the evolving role conceptualization of the principal. I argued the case that many schools lack the capacity to launch significant improvement efforts with a reasonable chance of success due to existing barriers and gaps which were highlighted (Glickman et al., 2010). These findings have implications for school districts and universities to examine issues of professional development, hiring practices, preparation, and university-district collaborations.

The existing systemic gaps observed as we engaged in our outreach efforts to provide professional development to school districts, facilitated the opportunity to direct our professional development efforts toward the practicing principals within one school district. The initial purpose was to build upon leaders' capacity within the district to effectively lead whole-school reform efforts they were charged to implement. A secondary outcome of the project, served to facilitate a sustained opportunity to contribute to the research centered on placing an increased emphasis on principal professional development, and the implications this has for university-district partnerships.

Chapter 2 expanded on the idea of university and school district partnerships as potentially being well situated to increase the learning, teaching, and leadership capacity of all levels of the educational system. Principals are currently expected to facilitate comprehensive school improvement efforts, frequently implementing the model of teacher professional learning communities to increase student achievement and meet the needs of diverse learners. However, many of these principals do not have experience in working with cultures of collaboration for the purpose of increasing student achievement. This chapter sets the stage for the need for principals' development and levels of support to align with the systemic innovations they are leading. This chapter highlights the changing role of university-district partnerships, as they work together to address existing gaps and opportunities for attaining mutually agreed upon outcomes. Also discussed, are the challenges and barriers presented when interdependent relationships are developed between two institutions characterized by differing cultures, expectations, and capacities. The conditions required to sustain the partnership in light of the differences and complex relationship are also addressed.

CHAPTER 2

UNIVERSITY-DISTRICT PARTNERSHIPS

CHAPTER OVERVIEW

Chapter 1 painted the contextual landscape of the external forces that have and continue to markedly change how the role of the principalship is currently conceptualized. This significant shift in thinking and in practice has had an astounding effect on universities, school districts and university-district partnerships. These two separate yet interdependent systems are challenged to examine ways to redefine their partnerships in an effort to meet the systemic challenges presented. This chapter addresses some of the ways that universities and school districts are revisiting their time-honored relationships and partnerships in response to the aftermath that has resulted in thinking differently about leadership; and consequently, expecting change from our leaders, the institutions who prepare them, and the school districts who hire them.

I have provided a brief historical overview of university-district partnerships, highlight the varying purposes of collaboration, and different models utilized to meet outcomes. I have paid specific attention to the ways that universities are rethinking their roles and pooling finite resources (Miller, Devin, & Shoop, 2007) to meet the changing needs of their students and constituents. I elucidated the opportunity to address a gap which I perceived existed in our emergent university-district partnership as I attempted to respond to the changing context. From this lens, I exposed the barriers and dynamics that intensify the complexity of university-district partnerships, and discuss the necessary conditions needed to sustain a complex partnership. I have embedded the research on these issues, but highlight the perspective gleaned from the experience and lessons learned from the 5-year project. The outcomes in this project centered on addressing a perceived gap within the pK20 pipeline, has implications for universities and district partnerships, as well as for building upon the findings in this research.

HISTORICAL ROLE OF UNIVERSITY AND SCHOOL-DISTRICT PARTNERSHIPS

Universities have long-standing interdependent relationships with school districts, as both systems are associated by mutual interest. Universities are historically known for teacher and principal preparation, as well as providing research-based best practices and theoretical frameworks for improving student performance (Miller et al., 2007). Consequently, schools provide real-world settings for application, analysis, evaluation, and monitoring of practices to improve student performance (Miller et al., 2007).

CHAPTER 2

The earliest university-district partnership can be traced back to the late 1800s when Charles W Eliot, president of Harvard, (Gooden, Bell, Gonzalez, & Lippa, 2011) created the "committee of ten." This early collaboration effort subsequently led to the development of the College Entrance Examination Board and the Scholastic Aptitude Tests (Gooden et al., 2005). Successive historical events led to the evolution of university-partnerships, and the emergence of various models, in an effort to respond to changing societal needs.

PROFESSIONAL DEVELOPMENT PARTNERSHIPS BETWEEN HIGHER EDUCATION AND PUBLIC SCHOOLS

There are different models and purposes for collaboration between the public schools and universities. Although partnerships can take a number of forms (Pace & Burton, 2003), the overarching goal is to integrate teaching and learning for the purpose of improving both (Holmes, 1986, 1990 in Pace & Burton, 2003). Burton and Patton (2003) asserted that advocates for educational systems change have encouraged the establishments of university/school district partnerships, also referred to as professional development schools (PDS). The concept of PDS originated with the Homes Group (1986, 1990 in Pace & Burton, 2003). The supporters of these partnerships posit that improved pre-service teacher education and in-service professional development are intended outcomes of this type of professional development reflective of the university-school district partnerships.

SIGNIFICANCE OF PARTNERSHIPS

An increasing body of literature supports the idea that the joining of forces between universities and school districts can be an effective approach for finding solutions to existing educational quandaries (Miller et al., 2007). Browne-Ferrigno and Sanzo, (2011) propose that a well-functioning university-district partnership supports the collaboration between leadership educators and leadership practitioners in ways that interactively enrich the field.

COMPLEXITY OF PARTNERSHIPS

Whereas the development of meaningful university partnerships continues to be a common interest of many higher education institutions, the building of significant partnerships, and overcoming the barriers is a complex task (Strier, 2011). Partnerships between the university and public schools are often very complex and vulnerable relationships. They are influenced not only by the personalities of the key partners, the cultures of the partners and the collaborative partnership, but also impacted by political decisions and the shared structures and processes needed for accomplishing project goals over time (Darling-Hammond, & McLaughlin (2003).

An important consideration when developing partnerships is that each entity has an understanding of the culture of both the university and the partnering district. In addition there must be a discussion of shared beliefs and agreement on non-negotiable tenets before the partnership is undertaken. However, if certain conditions are met and sustained, the mutual work between districts and universities serves to provide an opportunity for partners to not only achieve the project goals, but also begin to understand ways for building a community and co-constructing partnership systems for learning (Evans, 2001; Fullan, 2005).

CHALLENGES OF BRINGING TOGETHER TWO INHERENTLY DIFFERENT SYSTEMS

Two inherently different systems however, are not without hardship. Universities and districts are noted for their challenges as partnerships are difficult to create and sustain (Gooden et al., 2005). With respect to the challenges, university-district partnerships are urged to engage in collaborations, as research over the years supports the assertion that quality teaching and learning require collaboration (Comer, 1987 in Gooden et al., 2005). Browne-Ferrigno & Sanzo, (2011) reinforce this earlier finding by offering that neither universities nor districts can do what is needed on their own, neither can they single-handedly provide the breadth of experience needed to adequately develop and nurture leaders for today's pK-12 schools.

Given the inherent challenges that exist between combining two vastly different organizations (Myran, Sanzo, & Clayton, 2011), I make the case that purposeful university-district collaborations that work to establish and sustain necessary conditions, the university and the district can foster a culture of co-learners as put forward by Korach (2011).

CHANGED EXPECTATIONS AND NEW CHALLENGES FOR PARTNERSHIPS

In Chapter 1, I introduced the problem that because of the changed perceptual role and expectations held for today's school leader, many practicing principals may not have the current skills to fulfill these expectations. This paradigm shift in changed behaviors and in role expectations for both teachers and principals has a systemic impact on universities and school districts. Myran et al. (2011), suggest that the increase in accountability on both pK-12 districts and institutions of higher education has heightened the demands for partnerships between the two. It is important to underscore, that both systems are expected, challenged, and in some cases, even mandated or legislated (Browne-Ferrigno & Sanzo, 2011) to respond to externally imposed initiatives and innovations intended to improve conditions for teaching and learning. In this chapter, I will expand upon the idea that while these changes have complex implications for the pK-20 pipeline, they also present opportunities for building upon these initiatives as well as exploring new ideas that can address existing gaps.

CHAPTER 2

EXTERNAL FACTORS SERVING AS CATALYSTS FOR CHANGING LEADERSHIP PRACTICE

I characterize the effects of the changes felt by both systems by drawing attention to new practices and initiatives which have been informed by current literature and policy. The current way of thinking about teaching and learning has changed both the role perceptions of leaders, and has reconfigured leadership practices and expectations. While these changed paradigms create challenges as well as a sense of urgency for both systems to respond innovatively, the author provides specific examples of the practices and events that have facilitated universities and districts to revisit their partnerships to align more closely with new thinking about leadership. Also addressed, are the implications of these changes, which led to the university-district effort to respond to an existing gap which we perceived emerged as the aftermath of the changed contextual landscape.

UNIVERSITY-DISTRICT PARTNERSHIPS IN AN ERA OF ACCOUNTABILITY

The era of No Child Left Behind (NCLB), the most radical of reform efforts, has had a more subtle yet pervasive effect on universities than it has had on school districts. Further, the post NCLB literature and policy which continues to shape and influence how we think about teacher and leadership behaviors and roles, has created the need and urgency for universities to re-examine curriculum, internships and preparation programs. Universities are increasingly having to redefine how they partner with and engage school districts in response to these issues.

> To meet the needs of the 21st century, principal preparation programs may focus their programs on building leadership for second-order change, but without district and school support for the appropriate leadership, implementation of second-order change may be ineffective.
>
> Korach (2011)

SYSTEMS-THINKING

Change must be successful if schools are to achieve the ambitious goals of the 21st century (Korach, 2011). The demands and increased acceptance for whole-school reform efforts frequently require first-order and second-order systemic change to occur within the organizational context of school districts. This principle is often misunderstood or underestimated by many well-intended leaders and teachers, who are the recipients of programs, models, and initiatives intended to improve teaching and learning outcomes. This paradigm shift in thinking and in practice is placing pressure on universities to re-examine how universities prepare teachers and leaders, in context to the change in expected skills, behaviors, dispositions and attributes which are now expected.

In relation to understanding the systemic change process occurring in most school districts, and to a lesser extent in universities, it is important to understand the underpinnings of systems-thinking. The principles of systems-thinking are embedded in many whole-school reform models, as well as mandated state and federal initiatives. Briefly, theoretical literature on change presents the continuum of change, incorporating principles of technical and adaptive change. Technical change, corresponds with first-order change (Korach, 2011), where the norms of the system are not drastically affected. Conversely, adaptive or second-order change serves as the catalyst for challenging the assumptions, norms, beliefs, and time-honored practices of the organization. Korach (2011) asserts that the new learning needed to actualize the goals of No child Left Behind and to close achievement gaps requires second-order change to occur, which presents leaders and the complex organizational system with adaptive challenges.

McNamara (2007) synthesizes the phenomenon by explaining that if one part of the system is removed, the nature of the system is changed. Complex systems, such as school district organizations, are comprised of numerous subsystems, with each subsystem having its own boundaries, various inputs, processes, outputs, and outcomes geared to accomplish an overall goal for the subsystem. Systems-thinking provides a new perspective for leaders who are learning to look beyond the events to interpret the patterns and structures of the system and sub-systems in terms of the desired output of the whole system.

I purport that university-district partnerships whose collaborative purpose is to address the current educational challenges centered on the improvement of teaching and learning, will increasingly require university-district collaborations to implement change utilizing the principles of systems-thinking. The research centered on second-order change, advocates for a different-set of leadership skills required from those that guide technical change efforts (Waters et al., 2003 in Korach, 2011). As understood by researchers Heifetz, Grashow, and Linsky (2009 in Korach (2011), leaders who promote second-order change are "in the business of generating chaos, confusion, and conflict." Since the nature of second-order change serves to shift the status-quo, and alter the existing power structure, this type of leadership requires leaders who have exceptional skills with building relationships while promoting levels of ambiguity and tension.

I have made the supposition, that there is not a "critical-mass" of leaders in either system that are comfortable and adept in facilitating deep second-order change efforts. Further, this type of leadership, which needs to be cultivated and supported, requires sustained support from higher-levels of leadership within the system (Korach, 2011). I have interpreted the system as incorporating the pK-20 educational pipeline. These collective assertions provide continued opportunities for examining, re-defining and creating new university-district partnerships which may be better positioned to address these challenges as a collaborative system.

EMBEDDED TEACHER PROFESSIONAL DEVELOPMENT

Multiple educational researchers (DuFour, DuFour, & Eaker, 2008; National Association of Elementary School Principals [NAESP], 2012; Reeves, 2009; have

CHAPTER 2

become increasingly associated with the concept that professional learning of teachers that is job embedded and not conducted in isolation not only promotes school wide change, but also has an effect on student learning. Some authors such as Richards and Skolits, 2009) propose that the designing of effective and meaningful professional development for teachers needs to integrate experiential research in meaningful ways that can make evident the applicability to classroom instruction. Darling-Hammond and McLaughlin (2003) made a case for replacing traditional in-service requirements with job-embedded opportunities that foster knowledge sharing, based in context to specific learning and teaching experiences. It is essential that teachers are provided with opportunities to share what they know, discuss what they want to learn, and have multiple opportunities to connect new concepts and strategies to their own contexts (Darling-Hammond & McLaughlin, 2003). Many researchers uphold that tenets of teacher learning centered on changes in the knowledge, beliefs, and attitudes that lead to the attainment of new skills, concepts and processes are central to meaningful teacher professional development. Others have contributed to the research through their assertions that teachers need to be able to critically examine and reflect in their practice, attentive to the purpose of what they are doing and why.

Section 9101 of Tittle II in the NCLB Act requires that teachers' development be sustained through intensive training rooted in classroom practice, and that teachers and administrators develop, as well as evaluate (Mullen & Hutinger, 2008). The increasingly accepted view that replaces the old paradigm of delivering professional development to put in place the thinking advocated by the research corresponds closely with the premise that supports job-embedded teacher learning in both teams and collaboration (DuFour & Marzano, 2011). This shift in thinking and practice however, has direct implications for school leaders. They are both challenged and expected to have the skills and dispositions necessary for confronting teacher isolation, and for creating a learning culture that can support meaningful professional development which has the capacity of providing the expectation and continuous support to promote teacher growth and learning.

THE CASE FOR PROFESSIONAL LEARNING COMMUNITIES

Current best practices edified by prominent researchers in post NCLB educational literature, increasingly supports the position that teacher growth is promoted through learning facilitated in learning communities. The practice of moving teachers away from a culture of isolation, to a culture of collaboration, where continuous learning, shared practice, and job-embedded learning (Mullen & Hutinger, 2008) hold promise for affecting student achievement, has become the hallmark of learning communities.

> The far better strategy for improving adult practice is developing the results-oriented collaborative culture of a strong PLC, a culture committed to building the collective capacity of a staff to fulfill the purpose and priorities of their school or district. The focus must shift from helping individuals become

more effective in their isolated classrooms and schools, to creating a new collaborative culture based on interdependence, shared responsibility and mutual accountability.

DuFour & Marzano, 2011

Much can be inferred from the message embedded in this quote, which makes a poignant case for collaborative teacher learning, connecting the effects and impact of changed teacher behaviors and practices to the principal. Recent research on highly effective practices centered on teacher development (Carr, Herman, & Harris, 2005; DuFour & Marzano, 2011) supported and facilitated by school leaders, reported a correlation between teacher participation in collaborative learning communities to observed behavioral changes in collegial support, increased risk-taking, shared practice, improved levels of data analysis skills to inform instructional decisions, as well as a heightened focus on school improvement goals and outcomes.

LINKING THE ROLE OF PLCS TO TEACHER GROWTH AND PRINCIPAL RESPONSIBILITY

The post NCLB educational leadership literature is replete with findings that associate the responsibility of facilitating teachers' growth through collaborative learning communities with the role of the 21st century school leader. Although classroom teachers are considered the instruments of impacting direct student learning, multiple researchers (Evans, 2001; Fullan, 2005; Woolfolk Hoy & Kolter Hoy, 2006) continue to provide indication that the principal plays a paramount role in the success of teacher growth and embedded professional development.

Today's principals are expected to facilitate collaborative learning communities that provide evidence of fostering an environment where teachers construct knowledge and make meaningful connections (DuFour & Marzano, 2011; Ontario Principal's Council, 2009; Sergiovanni, 2006;) in job-embedded learning. Researchers are making the case that a PLC can span the scope of schools and school districts and embrace agencies and networks (Miller, et al., 2007), which are expected to include members from higher education, who are expected to modify their practices to affect teacher and learning outcomes.

As universities and school districts seek to capitalize on each other's strengths and resources for leadership development, one focus will continue to be on the development of quality, university-district partnerships.

Myran, Sanzo, & Clayton (2011)

THE ROLE OF PLCS IN A UNIVERSITY-DISTRICT PARTNERSHIP

Chapter 1 set the context of the changing role of the principal and the impact of national reforms, which continue to call for attention to be paid to the leadership role of school principals (Leithwood & Seashore-Louis, 2012). Federal, state, and local initiatives as well as findings informed by the educational literature influence the expectations and demands placed on the principal of the 21st century. The findings linking the role of the principal to facilitating teachers' growth in collaborative learning communities would unequivocally find its way to universities and university-district partnerships, as they share an interdependent relationship. Miller et al. (2007) support this overarching conceptualization by asserting that "leadership should be redefined around professional learning communities, which are described as team-based, cooperative arrangements between instructors and administrators." Advancing theories, beliefs, and politics centered on the changed role expectations of principals, has served to alter how universities are revisiting and adapting their roles with school-districts in an effort to meet these challenges.

> Though it may not be as extreme as what is happening in the pK-12 setting, there is increased accountability of university leadership preparation programs to be more effective and demonstrate this by measuring the impact their graduates have on student achievement.
> Gooden, Bell, Gonzales, & Lippa (2011)

UNIVERSITY-DISTRICT PARTNERSHIPS INVOLVED IN RE-DESIGN OF PRINCIPAL PREPARATION PROGRAMS

The focus on the skills and abilities of school principals and the quality of programs that prepare prospective school leaders has never been more intense (Davis & Darling-Hammond, 2012). One significant way in which universities are responding to the need to modify practices for affecting teaching and learning in an era of accountability is through the re-examination of how principals are being prepared. As a result, they are forging partnerships with school districts in the collaboration and re-design of principal preparation programs. Gooden, Bell, Gonzalez, and Lippa (2011) suggest that the appeal for a redesign of leadership preparation programs brings attention to the need for university-district partnerships as one part of a complex solution to increase the effectiveness of their programs. One of the greatest benefits of the collaborative partnership model is the partnership itself (Miller et al., 2007).

Multiple researchers on university-district partnerships highlight the inherent challenges to forming and sustaining partnerships where school-districts are given increasing voice in areas centered on curricular planning, internship design and a fundamental role in the redesign of principal preparation programs. The emergent research that reflects the stories, processes, research-based practices, and lessons learned as universities and districts forge partnerships centered on the co-development (Gooden et al., 2011) of principal preparation programs highlight common tenets which were found in frameworks that guided the work of effective partnerships.

CONCEPTUAL FRAMEWORK

A framework developed by the Southern Regional Education Board (SREB. 2008) features factors that are found in effective partnerships regardless of the models implemented between university-district partnerships. The factors that enable conditions for effective or highly functioning partnerships include:

1. Foster a common vision for the program, candidate learning and leadership outcomes;
2. Development of a shared commitment to the partnership, expressed through official written agreements and the allocation of resources (human and fiscal) to support the development and implementation of the program;
3. Clearly defining expectations for the roles and responsibilities of both parties;
4. Establish a process for gathering, analyzing and communicating formative and summative evaluation data to both parties;
5. Identify and ensure mutual benefits for both parties.

This framework, in addition to the research conducted on the conditions needed for effective university partnerships by researchers in the field highlighted in this chapter, served to guide our early and on-going efforts as a university-district partnership. Our partnership is not focused on principal preparation, but on sustained professional development geared to build leadership capacity to meet the expectations placed on the 21st century principal. The adherence to the principles of this framework has been invaluable to the partners at all stages of the partnership. The author addresses the application of the framework in context to the work of the partnership in subsequent chapters.

TWO TYPES OF PARTNERSHIPS RELEVANT TO OUR UNIVERSITY-DISTRICT PARTNERSHIP

Thus far, I have addressed the external conditions that have served as a call for university-district partnerships to re-examine the nature of their partnerships, providing potential opportunities to regroup and challenge assumptions and beliefs, expand and develop new innovations, in response to the changing context of education. It is important to highlight that there are several types of university-partnerships intended to serve a variety of purposes and outcomes. While the author does not expound on all of the various types of university-district partnerships, I briefly focus on the role of university-district partnerships in their effort to create Professional Development Schools. I also bring to the forefront the unique role of university-district partnerships in a rural context. These two types of university-district partnerships have specific significance to our 5-year partnership in two distinct, yet critical ways. The university-district partnership centered on creating professional learning communities, informs the aspects of our partnership centered on two institutions coming together to develop and sustain meaningful professional development through the creation of a professional learning community geared to

CHAPTER 2

focus on the development and support of practicing, site-based principals and school administrators.

The university-district partnership which explores the unique relationship between universities partnering with rural school districts is highly relevant to the context of our partnership. We are a state land-grant university, engaged in a university-district partnership with a rural school district. Therefore, providing a backdrop on the critical role of universities to partner in meaningful ways with rural school districts in the era of No Child Left Behind, serves to put additional context to our work and the momentum behind our efforts and collectively-shared sense of purpose.

> When a learning community has been developed through an effective PDS relationship, educational change can be effectively undertaken.
> Doolittle, Sudeck, & Rattigan, 2008

UNIVERSITY-DISTRICT PARTNERSHIPS—PROFESSIONAL DEVELOPMENT SCHOOLS (PDS)

Informed by recent educational literature, I have attempted to make the correlation between the underlying philosophy of professional learning communities and the role of the principal to facilitate effective professional learning communities. Therefore, it can be rationalized that if professional learning communities offer opportunities for improving the teaching and learning process (Doolittle, Sudeck, & Rattigan, 2008), then it can also be reasoned that the creation of strong professional development school (PDS) partnerships can establish an appropriate framework (Doolittle et al., 2008) for attaining that purpose.

PHILOSOPHY AND PURPOSE OF A PROFESSIONAL DEVELOPMENT SCHOOL

The underpinning of a PDS school is centered on student needs. A collectively shared sense of purpose that grounds the relationship between the university and district is that the university and school district faculty understand and value that learning, grounded in research and practitioner knowledge best occurs in a real-world setting (Doolittle et al., 2008). The researchers observed that in fully matured Professional Development Schools, university faculty have a noteworthy role in the school and strive to develop authentic relationships with faculty and staff, which support the reflection time needed between teachers and clinical teachers as they contemplate their observations and experiences (Doolittle et al., 2008).

The researchers observed that systemic change, as addressed in this chapter, plays a significant role in the purposing of a university-district partnership centered on the development of a professional development school. Doolittle et al. (2008) maintain the position that without intentionally pursuing systematic change, university PDS liaisons risk becoming glorified staff developers. These researchers underscore that by focusing on a mutually agreed-upon educational initiative and using a systemic change model real work can be accomplished and even sustained. The non-negotiable tenets of the university-district PDS partnership can be found in the framework that guides our project centered on building leadership capacity.

Although real change requires time for implementation, it is necessary to build capacity and deal with stakeholder concerns early on, when communicating and obtaining agreement about the intended outcomes of the partnership (Doolittle et al., 2008). This critical finding discussed by Doolittle et al. (2008) in their research, resonated closely with the philosophy of the partners and comprises one of the guiding principles of our work.

UNIVERSITY-DISTRICT PARTNERSHIPS WITH RURAL SCHOOL DISTRICTS

I have drawn attention to the numerous challenges fundamental to educational leaders who represent the pK-20 system, as they respond to the implications of the changing role of principal as manager to principal as instructional leader. For rural school districts, these challenges inherent in a post-NCLB era are exacerbated, and have specific significance for rural school principals. Rural school principals often see their most significant role as that of instructional leader, "but this is also the area where they feel they need the most significant professional development" (Browne-Ferrigno & Allen, 2006; Browne-Ferrigno & Knoeppel, 2005; Graham, Paterson, & Miller, 2008; Starr & White, 2008 in Myran et al., 2011). A study on rural principals completed in seven states by Salazar in 2007 (Myran et al., 2011) revealed that rural principals self-identified a critical need for professional development in building team commitment, creating learning organizations, sustaining and motivating for continuous improvement, and setting instructional direction. The principals in this study conveyed their overall sense of competence central to general management tasks. However, their sense of competence was not evident in the area of instructional leadership. The principals expressed that they did not feel they were prepared as instructional leaders. The conclusive outcomes of the study conducted by Salazar (2007 in Myran et al., 2011) suggest that the need for a strong instructional leader is paramount in rural districts, where teacher turnover is high and where the percentages of provisionally licensed teachers or teachers teaching out of their subject area is not uncommon practice (Myran et al., 2011). The findings of this study have profound implications for our university-district partnership intended to focus on building the instructional and overall capacity of the principals in this rural school district.

EXISTING GAP

I cautiously contend that the post-NCLB educational literature is becoming replete with best practices that facilitate teacher growth, linking teachers' development to the role of the principal. In this context, the principal is now charged with providing and facilitating learning environments conducive to promoting and fostering teachers' growth that can make a difference in the teaching and learning outcomes for students. As I have outlined, this task is undeniably complex, entailing far-reaching conditions that must be met. Researchers on university-district partnerships have provided criteria for frameworks that facilitate effective ways that universities and districts are responding to the challenges informed by the educational literature and educational policy. Because of the lack of published literature in the area of this topic, thee is additional opportunity to expound on the existing body of knowledge which informs practice.

The author received support from the Alliance at the university to further examine a perceived gap which could expound on the existing body of leadership literature. Since much of the literature is replete with findings that advocate for the new role expectations for principals, I observed an absence of sustained supports for practicing principals who are expected to meet the demands of the changed principal role. Universities and districts have developed collaborations that have facilitated the redesign of principal preparation programs as an important step to solving the problem that exists around developing prospective principals who reflect the attributes, skill-sets, and dispositions of what we now expect from today's principals.

From our perspective, an important next-step that we consider scant in the literature and in systematic practices of university-district partnerships is the focus on sustained professional development of practicing principals who may not have had the benefits of redesigned principal preparation programs.

THE THRESHOLD OF HIGHLY EFFECTIVE RE-DESIGNED PRINCIPAL PREPARATION PROGRAMS

It is an understatement that the partnership advocates for widespread practice of university-district partnerships, which are focused on the cultivation of interdependent relationships centered on the improvement of principal preparation programs. However, the refinement and revitalization of university principal preparation programs (National Conference of State Legislators [NCSL], 2008, *Senate Joint Memorial* [SJM]3), serves as one critical piece of the equation to the solution. In light of the most highly acclaimed principal preparation programs, several of my university colleagues propose that realistic expectations be placed on university preparation programs, to include university preparation programs that have been authentically co-designed with school districts.

Writing from the lens of a practicing professor genuinely invested in the high quality preparation of prospective school leaders, I have had the opportunity and privilege of partaking in a systematic state-wide effort designed to deeply examine the complex issues involved in the renewal of university principal preparation programs throughout our state. This extensive effort involved the participation of university and college faculty, college deans, superintendents, staff from state and legislative agencies, and members of the business community (NCSL, 2008, SJM 3).

Strong Leaders for New Mexico Schools: *Senate Joint Memorial 3: Report & Recommendations*—**A Report to the Legislative Education Study Committee**

The report was submitted to the New Mexico Legislative Education Study Committee (LESC) by the Office of Education Accountability (OEA), the Public Education Department (PED) and the Higher Education Department (HED) as required in *Senate Joint Memorial (SJM) 3: Recruitment and Preparation of Principals and Other School Leaders*. SJM 3 was unanimously passed in 2007 by the New Mexico Legislature, providing the initiative for the agencies of OEA, PED, and HED to commence collaborations with school districts and institutions of higher education, for the overarching purpose of developing a plan intended to enhance the recruitment, preparation, mentoring, evaluation, professional development and support for school principals and other educational leaders (*SJM* 3, 2008; Winograd, Garcia, & Dasenbrock, 2008).

Briefly, the report consisted of Six Recommendations and corresponding Action Steps:

1. Recommendation 1: Revitalize School Principal Standards
2. Recommendation 2: Strengthen Recruitment, Incentives and Retention
3. Recommendation 3: Develop and Implement the New Mexico Leadership Institute
4. Recommendation 4: Establish Data and Accountability Systems
5. Recommendation 5: Refine Current Certification Requirements
6. Recommendation 6: Refine and Revitalize University Principal Preparation Programs

I was honored to have worked with a team of colleagues who as exceptional leaders are representing higher-education, committed to taking action steps centered on Recommendation Six: The Refinement and Revitalization of University Principal Preparation Programs. The collaboration worked together to examine and take steps centered on the collaborative development of a core educational leadership curriculum designed to focus on what principals need to know and be able to do to improve student learning in pK-12 schools (*SJM* 3, 2008).

The culmination of this comprehensive 2- year effort, resulted in part, with agreed upon core courses containing course objectives and learning outcomes which were aligned to ISSLC Standards in addition to the NM Principal Leadership Competencies and Indicators. The final report was submitted to the LESC in December 2010. While the initiative has not been passed to date, the institutions collaborating on Recommendation Six, have respectively implemented tenets of the recommendations, to include redesigned core courses, embodied in this work. An important outcome of this work led to an Action Plan that has been implemented in our Department of Educational Leadership.

CHAPTER 2

REFLECTION ON THE COLLABORATION AND LESSONS LEARNED

This collaborative experience which brought to the table five diverse institutions of higher education representing the state was reflective of our shared sense of collective purpose, committed to the systematic improvement of principal preparation programs in our state. As we worked to determine the core courses and align objectives and outcomes of the core courses to the ISLLC Standards and to the NM Principal Leadership Competencies, two reoccurring themes were the basis of many of our conversations and deliberations that transpired over the span of two years.

Although there were several components outlined in Recommendation Six which were addressed, much deliberation and assessment in our efforts pertained to our selection and prioritization of objectives and learning outcomes that the team determined were of high priority, as they corresponded most closely to what was assessed that principals needed to know and be able to apply in order to be effective as 21st century principals leading schools in a complex context. The second theme which facilitated much consideration, planning, reflection, and negotiation, was the acknowledgement and process of coming to terms with, that in light of our collective expertise and best efforts to redesign our principal preparation programs, it is unreasonable to think that effective principal preparation programs will or have the capacity to teach all of the standards associated with effective school leaders. Walking away with this insight and sobering realization, served in part to build-upon my emergent premise that principals, even principals who have been fortunate to have graduated from high-quality programs that increase their ability to serve in a complex organizational context, are in need of sustained, systemic and differentiated professional development.

From this perspective, the author proposes that stakeholders who can embrace the concept of continuous learning, cultivating this belief through the sustained engagement in the context of a professional learning community designed to foster practices and behaviors which have been highlighted in these two chapters, will be better positioned to address the complex challenges informed by literature on best-practices and state and federal policy. The assertion has been made that continuous learning should include superintendents, central-office administrators, and university faculty.

UNSTAGED CAREER

A phenomenon that characterizes the career of teachers, and possibly to a lesser extent principals and superintendents, is what researchers refer to as the unstaged career (Glickman et al. 2010). Glickman et al., (2010) provide an example of a teacher's unstaged career from entry to exit of the profession. They propose that education majors take courses, spend time in schools, and perform as student teachers, and then graduate from college into their own classroom as teachers. The researchers bring to light that once the teacher begins to teach, regardless of the years spent teaching, the teacher has the same classroom space, number of students, and requirements of the first year teacher. While there are some differences between the career of the teacher and principal, this analogy can be applied to the principal's career, as the principal is frequently subjected to the similar quandary of a teacher's unstaged career.

The understanding of this phenomenon, in conjunction to the findings presented by the literature in both chapters, served to propel the implementation and further the examination of what sustained professional development meant to the principals when they learned more about instructional leadership and the complex role of the 21st century principal. The author was interested in gleaning their perspectives of the effect of learning with their peers on their role as principal.

CONCLUSION

The author has embedded the research that brought to the forefront the challenges of bringing together two vastly differing institutions for the purpose of increasing opportunities for learning and teaching that can change learning outcomes for students. I have also made the case that while university-district partnerships naturally have inherent challenges, university-district partnerships can purposefully work together to leverage their resources and natural strengths for attaining mutually agreed upon outcomes, when certain conditions are met, cultivated, and nurtured.

The events of external forces have irrefutably changed the contextual landscape of how we think about leadership and expect from the leadership role. There is an increasing sense of urgency for universities and districts to intentionally expand upon common ground for the purpose of building the capacity of both institutions to better meet the complex and diverse needs of students in the 21st century. I have delineated different ways that university-district partnerships are collaborating in an effort to meet this daunting charge. I have concluded this chapter by highlighting how the partners of this university-district collaboration identified an existing gap which we felt compelled to examine. The literature is replete with findings that advocate for the new role expectations for principals, which brought to light an absence of sustained supports for practicing principals who are expected to meet the demands of the changed principal role.

Chapter 3 provides a detailed account of the process, formation, and continuous development of our university-district partnership that facilitated the conceptualization of the Administrators' Professional Learning Community. As the Administrators' PLC developed and evolved throughout the 5-year partnership, conceptual frameworks and models were utilized to guide the emerging and developing work of the partnership. The maturation of the partnership led to the implementation and utilization of a variety of resources, as well as the development and refinement of frameworks that guided our work. Chapter 3 comprehensively addresses these processes, as well as the conditions that prompted us to adapt, revisit, and improve upon our practices.

CHAPTER 3

DEVELOPING THE MODEL FOR THE ADMINISTRATORS' PLC

As presented in the first two chapters, PLCs are increasingly gaining widespread acceptance as a system that can facilitate culture shifting (Matthews & Crow, 2010), holding increased promise of creating a culture committed to building the collective capacity of a staff to fulfill the purpose and priorities of their school or district (DuFour & Marzano, 2011). The DuFour Model of Professional Learning Communities (DuFour & Eaker, 1998), which embeds principles of systems change are increasingly implemented in school districts nationwide as an approach to facilitate whole-school reform efforts.

However, the research that sheds light on the voices of principals who understand that PLCs as an increasingly accepted practice of facilitating deep cultural and systemic change within the school organization is scant. It is the belief of the author that that there are fewer principals who have participated in PLCs as teachers, and even fewer principals who have participated in the change process evoked in participating in a Principals' PLC. The work that emerged as the result of the partnership between two institutions provided the opportunity to further the research through the implementation of an interpretive case study approach.

This chapter offers the process of the emergent and continuous development of the university-district partnership which facilitated the conceptualization of the Administrators' Professional Learning Community. As the Administrators' PLC developed and progressed throughout the 5-year partnership, a variety of resources, strategies, and approaches were utilized, developed, as well as modified to meet changing needs. This chapter conveys a description of the processes, the rationale for what was implemented and modified, and how this progression of implementation and refinement led to the continuous improvement process of the Administrators' PLC.

> The idea that principals should serve as instructional leaders—not just as generic managers—in their schools is widely subscribed to among educators. In practice, though, few principals act as genuine instructional leaders.
> Fink (2007)

Prior to my affiliation with the school district that has been fictitiously named the Southwest District, I was serving as a member of the Alliance, as part of my service and outreach efforts as a professor. A more compelling reason for serving with the Alliance is that I felt that the guiding principles of the Alliance closely aligned with my core values and beliefs, which were focused on my unwavering commitment to build leadership capacity in rural schools. In adherence to the mission and guiding principles of the Alliance, an outreach center at the university, the early stages of the collaboration between the Southwest School District and the Alliance was forged.

THE ALLIANCE FOR THE ADVANCEMENT OF TEACHING AND LEARNING (ALLIANCE)

Mission

The mission of the Alliance for the Advancement of Teaching and Learning is to collaboratively contribute to the success of children throughout New Mexico, with a primary focus on the southern part of the state, and the educators who serve them.

Vision

The vision of the Alliance is to serve as a catalyst for improved education for school personnel as well as children and families, particularly for those in rural and border areas in New Mexico. The Alliance collaborates with appropriate partners to meet the diverse needs of our children.

Goals

- To be the principal academic entity providing comprehensive training and educational consulting services to New Mexico schools, particularly rural schools.
- To be the catalyst and inspiration for all schools to meet and exceed the expectations outlined consistent with the requirements of the Elementary and Secondary Education Act, evolving New Mexico Statutory requirements, strategic planning and the Educational Plan for Student Success (EPSS).

Objectives

- To provide teachers, administrators, parents, and children access to materials that will improve academic progress and success.
- To collaborate with the Public Education Department (PED) and Regional Educational Cooperative Centers (REC) to provide training and consulting services to schools, particularly rural schools.
- To work with identified schools to assist them in achieving alignment between the Educational Plan for Student Success, Instruction, and Student Outcomes.
- To provide additional resources for identified areas (e.g., reading, science, math, special education, and bilingual education).
- To conduct formative and summative evaluation of collaborative initiatives implemented to address the goals of the Alliance and to statistically evaluate best practices for improving the education of children in schools.

- To disseminate information and research about best practices in meeting the challenges of schools.
- To advise and assist school districts and schools in the development of family involvement policies and procedures that facilitate and sustain family involvement that is consistent with the requirements of the Elementary and Secondary Education Act, evolving New Mexico Statutory requirements, strategic planning and the Educational Plan for Student Success (EPSS).

THE EARLY PHASE OF THE COLLABORATION

In the emergent stages of the collaboration, prior to the transformation into the partnership (Browne-Ferrigno, 2011), the services provided by the university were in the form of technical support intended to build capacity of teachers and principals in using data to inform instructional practice. In the research conducted by Browne-Ferrigno (2011), the distinction between a collaboration and university-district partnership is delineated. The assertion is made that in more "tightly coupled" arrangements more closely reflective of partnerships, professors and practitioners work together to develop curriculum, deliver instruction and assess learning progress in the context of learning-oriented and reality-based practices (Billet, 1996; Martin & Papa, 2008; & Smith, 2003 in Browne-Ferrigno (2011).

The attributes that are associated with a partnership were evidenced after the implementation of the Administrators' PLC. It was within that context which afforded the university professor who serves as the facilitator of the PLC, to work closely with central office administrators and the site-based principals to engage in activities that include the development of curriculum, the assessment of learning, and the engagement of continuous learning, as it correlates with determined district and site-based outcomes. The Administrators' PLC was not put into implementation until the second year of the partnership.

> Based on what we know about successful schools, the time has come to move from conventional schools and congenial schools toward collegial schools.
> Glickman, Gordon, Ross-Gordon (2010)

DEVELOPING A COLLEGIAL SCHOOL CULTURE

Over-time, the attributes of the emerging collaboration evolved into a university-district partnership. As the vision to change the existing practices to a culture that reflected the characteristics of a collegial school culture (Glickman et al., 2010) the priorities of the stakeholders changed. Briefly, a collegial school culture as described by Glickman et al. (2010), is a school that makes learning a priority through the establishment of learning goals for all students to support the charge of education in a democratic society. These researchers affirm that collegial schools are always studying teaching and learning, setting common priorities, making decisions about internal changes and resource allocations, and assessing effects on student learning Glickman et al. (2010).

SENSE OF URGENCY TO FOCUS ON PRINCIPAL PROFESSIONAL DEVELOPMENT

The need to build principal leadership capacity became the immediate priority. It was agreed upon that the structures and interventions that were put into place would have limited efficacy and hold little promise for sustainability if the principals did not buy into the change, have the instructional skills and capacity to guide teachers' development, or were not able to maximize the use of interventions and structures that the district provided.

ADEQUATE YEARLY PROGRESS

After two years of continuous and aligned work grounded in research based practices system-wide, the efforts of the university-district partnership resulted in considerable gains on Adequate Yearly Progress (AYP) designations district-wide. Most of the schools made AYP in both math and in reading on the additional indicators in the AYP report.

It is important to mention that as of 2012, schools in New Mexico receive a District Report Card, which provides a designated grade for each school. The State Report Card provides a summary of AYP ratings, proficiency attendance and graduation statistics at the school level; proficiency statistics for all students' demographics, expenditures, and the parent survey on quality of education at the state level (NMPED, 2012). An in-depth discussion that provides a rationale for the changed system that measures progress, the implications it has for school districts, principals and teachers, as well as the findings obtained from the 5- year project, is addressed in the final chapters of this book.

> Schools will not improve unless the administrators and teachers within them improve.
>
> Wise, (1991)

This overarching tenet has been firmly embedded in the framework that guides the work of the partnership between the Southwest School District and the University. The partnership has commenced its fifth year, bound by a shared and unwavering vision and deep commitment to building leadership capacity for leading and facilitating change in the organizational culture.

As the partnership cultivated the shared vision, we determined that the system will not make sustainable improvement reflected in student achievement unless school renewal is addressed systemically. It was also agreed upon that leadership matters, and is essential for building teacher capacity and for changing the organizational culture that embraces continuous improvement evidenced in student-centered practices. This thinking led to the implementation of the Administrators' Professional Learning Community, which is now in its fourth year. A purposeful outcome of this model is that leaders will become more intentional and skillful in helping their teachers to become increasingly connected with teaching and with their students' learning.

ADMINISTRATORS' PLC CONCEPTUAL FRAMEWORK

The conceptual framework has been designed to build upon leadership capacity for the vision of developing and sustaining strong instructional school leaders who are capable of leading systemic school renewal that provides evidence of increasing school and district-wide student achievement. A unique feature of this framework embodies the innovation of creating and sustaining an Administrators' Professional Learning Community (PLC), embedded in the belief that schools will not systemically improve without the improvement of school principals and administrators. The focus of this learning community was designed, developed, and refined for meeting the Administrators' needs within the district.

The principals in this learning community have continuous opportunities to practice, reflect, and assess their skills and leadership behaviors that research suggests affect teacher behaviors and student achievement. Another element of this framework is the overarching model that involves the sustained work between the university and school district, working interdependently and systemically to share resources for the purpose of implementing and sustaining the model as it aligns to the underlying principles of the framework.

As delineated in Chapter 1, the assertion was made that while there is more than one model of a PLC, recent research contributing to the PLC literature suggests that there are common cultural elements found in the framework of most effective PLC models (Matthews & Crow, 2010). In developing the models that were proposed and used, the facilitator, working closely with the associate superintendent and principals, relied on these elements as a form of continuous assessment. This practice provided indication as to where increased focus needed to occur, or where modifications needed to be made.

In any continuous improvement process, some tenets will pose significantly more challenging than other elements. The element: *Academic Success for All Students with Systems of Prevention and Intervention* (Matthews & Crow, 2010) was and continues to be, a primary focus of the systemic work of the university-district partnership. Without adherence to a conceptual framework, it would have made it much more difficult to assess the progress of the learning community, in correlation to the mission and vision that guided our work.

CHAPTER 3

CULTIVATING A COLLECTIVE MISSION AND SHARED SENSE OF PURPOSE

An integral tenet that guided the conceptual framework was the cultivation of a collective mission and shared sense of purpose, where evidence of shared-leadership practices were valued and implemented. While our mission was not solidified during our first year as an Administrators' PLC, the intention to cultivate and solidify our mission, vision, and shared sense of collective purpose was prevalent in our early work. We now have a finalized PLC definition that reflects the voices of the principal participants and the teachers throughout the district. However, it is imperative to underscore that this was not an easy task to accomplish, as attaining a collective sense of ownership in a school culture where isolation was a prominent characteristic, required a focused, multi-year effort to solidify.

DuFour, DuFour, and Eaker (2008) speaks to the quandary involved in the process of developing a collectively shared vision, suggesting the strategy of co-creation. While these researchers assert that the co-creating strategy may not be the most efficient way to develop a written vision statement, it is the strategy likely to result in the shared vision critical to a learning community (DuFour, DuFour, & Eaker, 2008).

OUR COLLECTIVE DEFINITION OF A PROFESSIONAL LEARNING COMMUNITY

A Professional Learning Community Is:

✓ *A group of interdependent educational professionals with a common purpose focused and committed to the learning of <u>every individual</u> to improve* **Student Achievement.**
✓ *A structure which allows teachers, staff, and administrators to effectively collaborate and share learned practices to address and reflect on core components of* **Curriculum, Instruction,** *and* **Assessments.**
✓ *A platform for teachers, staff, and administrators to come together to make data informed decisions and put in place* **interventions** *which impact student learning.*
✓ *A forum for professional growth that facilitates discussion and action around* **implementation** *and* **continuous learning.**

The SREB Leadership Curriculum Models are changing the way school leaders are trained by guiding the redesign of preparation programs and professional development.

Southern Regional Education Board (SREB, 2008)

SREB

The conceptual framework of the Administrators' Professional Learning Community is grounded in the ISLLC Standards, NAESP Standards and in the 13 Critical Success Factors developed by the Southern Regional Educational Board (2008), which determine the skills sets, dispositions and attributes of what leaders who serve as change agents "should know and be able to do (SREB, 2008)." The 13

Critical Success Factors comprise the framework for SREB training modules. These factors have been identified in SREB studies of principals contributing to school and classroom practices that increase student achievement (SREB, 2008).

THE SREB CRITICAL SUCCESS FACTORS

1. **Focusing on Student Achievement:** Create a focused mission to improve student achievement and a vision of the elements of school, curriculum and instructional practices that make higher achievement possible.
   - Successful leaders have a very targeted mission to improve student achievement. They have a vision of the school as a place that makes a difference in the lives of students, and they value every student in their present and future world. Middle school leaders believe their primary mission is to get students ready to succeed in challenging high school studies, and high school leaders see as their primary mission preparing students to make a successful transition to postsecondary studies and work.
   - School leaders need a deep and comprehensive understanding of changes in curriculum, instruction, school practices and organization that will produce gains in student achievement. Successful school leaders reject "one-shot" projects that do not fit seamlessly into a larger improvement initiative. School leaders should have sufficient knowledge about research-based school and classroom practices to develop or adapt, with the involvement of faculty, a set of guiding principles and goals that keep them focused on student learning. All school principals need to know how school leaders who have improved achievement in low-performing schools were able to get the faculty, students and parents to buy into the belief that being "smart" is based on effort and hard work and is not limited to students at the top of the ability chart.

2. **Developing a Culture of High Expectations:** Set high expectations for all students to learn higher-level content.
   - Successful school leaders understand that increasing academic rigor and eliminating low-level courses have a positive impact on student achievement. They know how to use study groups to engage faculty, parents and others to give more students access to demanding courses with a minimum of social tension by proving it can be done. Leaders who have realized significant gains in student achievement made college-preparatory/honors classes the standard for all students. They are committed to providing schools where all students succeed and where all students have access to high-level content.

> Educational leaders need to know how to help their teachers share the belief that all students can learn what their schools have previously taught only to their best students. Exemplary leaders use meetings, discussions, staff development activities, interviews with former students, visits to other schools and data to help faculty become dissatisfied with a system that does not educate all students well and to develop ideas about changes the school can make to raise the achievement of all students. As leaders, they help parents, teachers and even community members who are accustomed to the labeling and sorting of students to find value in giving more students access to demanding courses.

3. **Designing a Standards-Based Instructional System:** Recognize and encourage implementation of good instructional practices that motivate students and increase student achievement.
   > Future school leaders need deeper knowledge of content fields and instructional methods that motivate and engage students and connect subject matter content to real-world problems and projects. Well-prepared principals know how to select effective professional development for their schools, evaluate high-quality instruction, and understand and support teachers as they struggle to learn new ways of teaching.
   > School principals for the future must be well-versed in national, state and local standards and the curriculum and instructional methods that can help students meet standards. They must give leadership and support to teachers in aligning teacher assignments, student work and classroom assessment to higher content and performance standards. As school leaders deepen their knowledge of research-based instructional methods and classroom assessment, they will become skillful at keeping a constant focus on quality classroom instruction. They will be prepared to support a variety of successful practices, such as making observations, asking probing questions of students and teachers, and creating a setting for teachers to share their successes (and failures) with each other.
   > Future school leaders must use the computer and the Internet to enhance their own learning. Beyond that, they need to understand how technology can engage students in learning, what a classroom looks like when technology has been successfully integrated into instruction, and how to support teachers in learning how to use technology to advance student achievement.

4. Creating a Caring Environment: Develop a school organization where faculty and staff understand that every student counts and where every student has the support of a caring adult.
- ➤ School leaders need to know how to organize a school to achieve a personalized learning environment where every student counts and has a personal relationship with a caring adult. All students are more motivated to learn in such a setting.
- ➤ Successful leaders work in schools of various sizes, but these leaders always establish some way to personalize learning. If the school is large, they are aware of the research on "small learning communities" and they reorganize to create schools within-a-school. They have an advisor-advisee system so that every student has an adult mentor in the building who can help him or her to learn about options, set goals, choose courses and get extra assistance to meet course standards. The advisor-advisee process promotes intense parent involvement in supporting students to meet their present and post-high school goals. Successful leaders get parents to visit the school with their children at least once a year for an advisement session.

5. Implementing data-based improvement: Use data to initiate and continue improvement in school and classroom practices and student achievement.
- ➤ The literature is clear on this matter. Collecting, understanding and using a wide variety of data are crucial leadership skills in these times of accountability. Successful school leaders must be adept at leading their faculty in action research and in using technology to analyze data. They know how to disaggregate data and connect assessment results to school and classroom effectiveness.
- ➤ Future leaders need to understand how to use data as a discussion tool for reshaping the attitudes of teachers, parents and students about changing course offerings and instructional strategies. Principals in schools that have made significant improvement in student achievement did not hide bad news but used data as a tool to get people to take ownership of the problems and to do something about them. School leaders must have the persistence and courage to change a faculty mind-set that everything in their school is fine. When change is mentioned in some schools, teachers exclaim, "This can't be done." Persistence in the use of meaningful data will eventually result in new behaviors and higher student achievement.
- ➤ Principals need to understand how to present data to faculty and parents in a format that is understandable and clearly defines courses of action. This includes disaggregating data to show where the weaknesses are—by standards and by different groups of students. Successful leaders use data to make decisions about school and classroom practices and to provide curriculum interventions for students.

- Successful leaders go beyond student achievement data to look at school practices, what students are taught, how they are taught and what is expected of them. They use data to prove to their faculty that low-achieving students have been exposed to inadequate schooling experiences and need a more rigorous curriculum and more engaging learning experiences to catch up. Research verifies that, in schools where teachers analyze data and study research about teaching methods that have proven successful for students, more effective instructional strategies emerge in the classrooms.
- Successful schools that are "data-driven" rely on many sources of information, including student feedback, instruments that measure student progress and statistics that are collected formally and informally.
- Successful leaders do not wait for data from the "big tests." They support teams of teachers to collect and analyze students' work against performance standards, to use common end-of-grading period exams and collectively study the results, to prepare common scoring guides and apply them to students' work, and to help guide instruction on a day-to-day basis. Future leaders need to understand that it is hard to know if you are making progress if you do not measure along the way.

6. **Communicating:** Keep everyone informed and focused on student achievement.
   - Exemplary school leaders are very visible in their schools. They spend the majority of their time in classroom with the teachers and students. Their actions communicate a belief system that principals should stay in touch with the classroom and dedicate their time to curriculum, instruction and issues of teaching and learning. They must have a clear message that constantly communicates to everyone about the things that matter the most to student achievement:

     - Providing demanding courses and engaging assignments;
     - Getting smart by working hard;
     - Helping students make sense out of what they are asked to do; and
     - Giving students needed extra assistance to meet course standards.

   - Effective communication is the cornerstone of a school wide focus on student achievement. And the definition of "effective communication" is changing. In many schools, the traditional newsletters, presentations at civic club meetings, and mailings have been replaced with Web sites, electronic distribution lists, group e-mails and listserv discussions. The work of a leader at the highest level is to use personal contacts and technology to lead the conversation about what is essential and what is not.

> Future leaders must understand the need to create opportunities for themselves and their faculty to communicate with teachers, leaders and parents from feeder schools about rising standards and expectations, and about what entering students need to know and be able to do. At the same time, they need to create opportunities for themselves and their faculty to get feedback about their strengths and deficiencies from schools that receive their students.

7. **Involving Parents:** Make parents partners in their student's education and create a structure for parent and educator collaboration.
   > There are documented positive relationships between high parental involvement and high student achievement. The school leaders who reported that they reached out and involved parents had schools with higher student achievement. Successful involvement includes a deep and intense effort on the part of the school to parents in many aspects of the education of their children. This may mean sending staff to a student's home to explain how the school operates, asking parents to sign a learning contract, or establishing community and family traditions that encourage school involvement.
   > Successful leaders make parents partners and create a structure for parents and educators to work together. For example, in high school they build long-term plans for students that outline four years of high school and two years beyond. Successful leaders are committed to telling parents the truth about their children's progress. They explain that in order for students to succeed, there must be shared ownership of any problem. Parents will know what the school will do, what they must do, and what the students must do to produce higher student achievement. Successful leaders understand that the school cannot do it alone, and they understand how to get teachers, parents and students to work with them. This support benefits the students and results in more students taking more challenging courses and achieving at a higher level.

8. **Initiating and Managing Change:** Understand the change process and have the leadership and facilitation skills to manage it effectively.
   > Future school leaders need to understand how to provide their staff with experiences and conditions that will create dissatisfaction with the current level of student achievement and with current school and classroom practices. Successful leaders encourage meaningful discussion and dialogue focused on the education of the student—even if it generates different ideas and conflicts. Study groups and discussion groups are part of the staff development program.

CHAPTER 3

> ➤ Effective principals understand that change occurs when other school leaders agree there is a problem and take ownership for it and for the solution. Part of the process of being an effective school leader is understanding how to organize, lead and facilitate experiences that result in consensus among the faculty, parents and community leaders. Leaders need opportunities to gain broad knowledge of "change" literature in education and other settings, to study case studies of effective school change, to observe and participate firsthand in such experiences, and to have their own leadership and facilitation skills critiqued.
> ➤ Further, future leaders need to know how to orchestrate an array of experiences that result in more staff changing their beliefs about how much some students can learn. Through these experiences, the staff gains insights into how to raise expectations and teach a demanding curriculum to more students. Successful leaders challenge people in a way that requires changes in their priorities, their values and their habits. It is never comfortable to be a lightning rod, but successful school leaders understand how to deal with the change process. They are persistent and decisive and they take action.
> ➤ School leaders must learn how to separate "skeptical resisters" from "professional resisters." They need to know how to identify the "skeptical resisters" and involve them in thinking about the best ways to implement a major change. And they must learn how to prevent the "professional resisters" from becoming a barrier to major school improvement.
> ➤ Successful leaders are not afraid to involve others in meaningful discussion and dialogue about change and to earn their "buy-in." Because they are true leaders, they have the ability to take people where they would not go alone. In the process, they build schools that support greater student learning.

9. Providing Professional Development: Understand how adults learn and know how to advance meaningful change through quality sustained professional development that benefits students.
> ➤ Leaders need to understand how to tie professional development to a school improvement plan; make it ongoing; and provide professional development opportunities that will make a difference in student achievement. They make sure teachers are well-trained in new instructional methods and the effective use of "blocks" of instructional time. They create a strong support system for new teachers that orients them to the school's vision and provides long-term mentoring.

DEVELOPING THE MODEL FOR THE ADMINISTRATORS' PLC

- ➤ Future leaders must know how to get beyond the traditional passive model for staff development that relies primarily on one-shot afternoon speakers and travel to professional conferences. They need to gain skills in leading a community of learners and must serve as models of professional "life-long learners" themselves. They must know how to support staff developments through study groups, problem-solving sessions and regular meetings to discuss students' needs. To ensure continuous professional growth in the school, the successful principal must develop a network of teacher mentors and master teachers who can serve as on-site staff developers. Leaders who know how to give faculty the time and opportunity to adjust and learn new strategies and plan for follow-through will create a school where everyone is always improving.
- ➤ Exemplary leaders are committed to making the most of every professional development opportunity. Rather than send one or two individuals to a conference, they take a team that might include the principal or other key leaders from the staff. They will organize a time at the conference for the team to meet and share what they have learned and to plan what they can share and implement at their school that will improve student achievement. This is a powerful model, because when the team returns to the school, it takes ownership of the ideas and supports their implementation.

10. **Innovating:** Use and organize time in innovative ways to meet the goals and objectives of school improvement.
    - ➤ Future leaders cannot be prisoners of time. They must know about and advocate a variety of scheduling models that promote extended school days, extended school years, tutorial programs, innovative summer school programs and other methods to increase time for student achievement. "Time" must be seen by everyone as an important commodity that makes it possible for faculty to discuss students' needs, improve instruction and align classroom assignments and students' work to higher standards.
    - ➤ Successful leaders know that teachers must spend more time planning classroom instruction if they are going to help all students achieve at higher levels. Teachers have to plan instruction that goes beyond the textbook if they are to add relevancy to lessons and convince more students that the learning they are being asked to master is important.
    - ➤ Successful leaders also know that some students need extra time and support to meet standards. They provide that time through a variety of methods like tutoring, extra sessions during breaks, and summer school. One leader rearranged summer school so that each student was assigned to a teacher for special tutoring. Teachers had no more than five students each and the freedom to schedule help for students as needed.

CHAPTER 3

> ➤ Effective principals do not water down the curriculum or slow the pace but use extra time and support to help students meet course standards. They believe that effort is a far greater indicator of success than ability and believe, given enough time and support, that most students can achieve at high levels. They use time to promote a continuous improvement model for their students and their schools.
> ➤ The successful school leaders we interviewed were not willing to lose instructional time to interruptions, athletic events, pep rallies, teachers' meetings or extracurricular activities. Instructional time was guarded. One principal saw that excessive use of the intercom was eating up precious classroom instructional time. She also realized that the school's Friday prom schedule curtailed instructional time, because students checked out early or did not come to school on prom Friday. She eliminated the use of the intercom, changed the prom to Saturday, and refocused her school on the necessity of giving instructional time the highest priority.

11. **Maximizing Resources:** Acquire and use resources wisely.
    > ➤ Future leaders must be entrepreneurs, with the knowledge and skills to secure needed resources from a variety of sources. With the help of faculty, they need to know how to write grants or develop partnerships with businesses, universities, and community agencies.
    > ➤ Exemplary leaders will not wait for someone else to provide what may be needed to improve their schools. They are constantly searching for dollars to support staff development, technology, time for teachers to plan, curriculum alignment, Saturday morning tutorials, make-up classes and summer transition programs. Some leaders we interviewed even made arrangements with a colleague to support the statistical analysis of their performance data. The list is almost endless. These leaders essentially search for resources that support anything that helps students achieve. Technology is especially important to these leaders, since it is not just a management tool for them but a teaching and learning tool for their teachers and students.

12. **Building External Support:** Obtain support from the central office and from community and parent leaders for their school improvement agenda.
    > ➤ Future leaders need to understand how to develop key "champions" for their improvement agenda. They can do this by continuously sharing with parents and community leaders meaningful information about: the current state of student achievement and of school and classroom practices; what the school is doing to improve; how parents and the community can help; and the progress being made. Learning how to use key central office staff and community and parent leaders as friendly critics and advisors in developing and carrying out an improvement agenda can provide leaders with key spokespersons in the larger community.

> ➢ Exemplary leaders develop relationships with central office personnel who give them the necessary support for their improvement agenda. They nurture allies among community and parent leaders who provide critical support when things become confrontational. One principal who fostered a non-traditional schedule was confronted with a board that wanted return to a traditional high school schedule. The principal never did address the problem, because the community, already aware of the success the school was having with the schedule, protested and the issue as dropped.

---

13. **Staying Abreast of Effective Practices:** Continuously learn and seek out colleagues who keep them abreast of new research and proven practices.
    ➢ Learning from exemplary leaders, is an ongoing endeavor and they model lifelong learning to their teachers. They create ongoing professional conversations among their peers in their own school systems. They establish relationships with a variety of professional groups and with organizations like High Schools That Work (HSTW), the Coalition of Essential Schools, New American High Schools and the National Forum to Accelerate Middle Grades Reform, to name a few. They find that these networks give them a comprehensive set of key practices that they and their teachers can use as a framework for school improvement. These networks provide access to resources and opportunities to learn from other schools.

Alignment of the SREB Success Factors to the NM HOUSSE-P Evaluation System

The 13 Critical Success Factors were also aligned to the Domains found in the New Mexico HOUSSE-P Evaluation system used to evaluate principals (Ludeke, 2010).

Domain: *Instructional Leadership*

Competency 1: The principal promotes the success of all students by maintaining a culture that supports student achievement, high quality instruction, and professional development to meet the diverse learning needs of the school community.

Aligns with Critical Success Factor(s)

Critical Success Factor 1: Create a focused mission to improve student achievement and a vision of the elements of school, curriculum and instructional practices that make higher achievement possible.

Critical Success Factor 2: Set high expectations for all students to learn higher-level content.

CHAPTER 3

Critical Success Factor 3: Recognize and encourage implementation of good instructional practices that motivate students and increase student achievement.

Critical Success Factor 5: Use data to initiate and continue improvement in school and classroom practices and student achievement.

Critical Success Factor 9: Understand how adults learn and know how to advance meaningful change through quality sustained professional development that benefits students.

Domain: Communication

Competency 2: The Principal uses communication and relationship-building skills to engage the larger community in the knowledge of and advocacy for equity in meeting the diverse needs of the school community.

Aligns with Critical Success Factor(s):

Critical Success Factor 4: Create a school organization where faculty and staff understand that every student counts and where every student has the support of a caring adult.

Critical Success Factor 6: Keep everyone informed and focused on student achievement.

Critical Success Factor 7: Make parents partners in their student's education and create a structure for parent and educator collaboration.

Critical Success Factor 8: Understand the change process and have the leadership and facilitation skills to manage it effectively.

Domain: Professional Development

Competency 3: The Principal organizes and coordinates ongoing professional learning opportunities that are aligned with the New Mexico Professional Development Framework and supports the diverse learning needs of the school community.

Aligns with Critical Success Factor(s):

Critical Success Factor 5: Use data to initiate and continue improvement in school and classroom practices and student achievement.

Critical Success Factor 9: Understand how adults learn and know how to advance meaningful change through quality professional development that benefits students.

Critical Success Factor 13: Continuously learn and seek out colleagues who keep them abreast of new research and proven practices.

Domain: Operations Management

Competency 4: The Principal manages the school campus, budget, and daily operations to equitably meet the diverse learning needs of the school community.

Aligns with Critical Success Factor(s):

Critical Success Factor 10: Use and organize time in innovative ways to meet the goals and objectives of school improvement.

Critical Success Factor 11: Acquire and use resources wisely.

Critical Success Factor 12: Obtain support from the central office and from community and parent leaders for their school improvement agenda.

Domain: Scope of Responsibility in Secondary Schools

Competency 5: The middle school and high school Principal develops, supports, encourages, and supervises programs that lead to increased student attendance, achievement, and graduation rates resulting in college readiness and work skills to meet the diverse needs of the community.

Aligns with Critical Success Factor(s):

Critical Success Factor 4: Create a school organization where faculty and staff understand that every student counts and where every student has the support of a caring adult.

Critical Success Factor 5: Use data to initiate and continue improvement in school and classroom practices and student achievement.

Critical Success Factor 7: Make parents partners in their student's education and create a structure for parent and educator collaboration.

Critical Success Factor 11: Acquire and use resources wisely.

Critical Success Factor 13: Continuously learn and seek out colleagues who keep them abreast of new research and proven practices.

EMERGING MODEL

The emerging model that was established to operationalize the framework entailed two bi-monthly Administrators' PLCs that required the attendance of the university facilitator, the associate superintendent, site-building principals, and central office administrators. The district superintendent made a concerted effort to actively partake in these Administrators' PLCs, as part of his commitment to support the shared-principle that the active participation of each member is critical to the on-going learning and continuous improvement process. The activities and intentional conversations were centered on the elements embedded in the framework, focused

CHAPTER 3

on providing aligned and continuous support for principals who can lead effective Professional Learning Communities at their respective sites.

This systemic innovation is supported by the district in an effort to facilitate a collegial learning culture that corresponds to higher-levels of student-achievement, reinforced by leadership literature and research-based best practices. As will be discussed in the final chapters, this district experienced a succession of three district office superintendents since the commencement of the early collaboration. Without the unwavering support of the associate superintendent, and collectively shared vision of the university facilitator, sustainability of this conceptualization and focus would have been highly improbable. It is important to mention that since the conceptualization of the Administrators' PLC, the current superintendent, participates in the PLC on a regular basis.

EVOLVING MODEL

The data collected and synthesized in bi-monthly reports has been used to guide the subsequent sessions over the past four years. Further, the analyses of this data have provided substantive evidence that a paradigm-shift in thinking and in practice has occurred with the members of the Administrators' PLC. The findings obtained from the principals' voices from the 5-year project are revealed in subsequent chapters.

An integral part of our approach based on the core beliefs and guiding principles as a university-district partnership is to put into practice continuous assessment, collaboration and discussions, and the ability to make modifications and adjustments to the delivery of the model. These tenets are implemented in part of a concerted effort to meet the changing developmental needs of the participants as it aligns to district and school outcomes. This extensive process led to the implementation of an individualized and differentiated coaching model used to provide support for the Administrators' PLC Framework and Model.

> MENTORING, COACHING, AND COLLABORATION ARE SHARED PROCESSES. A shared journey of commitment to effective practice and improved learning for all students. In a learning community, adults and children alike are learners as they experiment, give and receive feedback, and use and offer support. When these interactions are embedded in the school culture, a new synergy evolves and a shift occurs—a shift to the forward momentum of collaborative school renewal.
>
> Carr, Herman, & Harris (2005)

INDIVIDUALIZED COACHING TO PRINCIPALS

During the third year of the university-district-partnership, and the second year of the Administrators' PLC, the principals expressed a collective interest in receiving additional support which spanned the scope of the learning delivered in the context of the Administrators' PLC. The principals asked for differentiated support to align with their varied developmental stages, in addition to the specific issues, needs and challenges inherently unique to their respective school sites. The principals received an hour to an hour-and-half of individualized coaching at their respective school sites, delivered bi-monthly by the university facilitator.

The university facilitator perceived this request to receive additional support as one indicator that the principals' sense of urgency to address their own levels of efficacy as instructional leaders had been piqued. Another important indicator that was gleaned pertained to the internalization process that was occurring. Observed at varying degrees, the principals were becoming increasingly intentional about putting into practice what was learned. Of equal importance, the principals were motivated to link the learning and put it into practice, in perspective to their school's cultural context, considering the needs of their teachers, students, and the community in which they served.

LIMITED RESOURCE CAPACITY AND SUSTAINABILITY OF COACHING

Issues of capacity pertaining to allocation of very limited resources of time and money were imminent. The university-district project was funded by a grant awarded to the Alliance, and supplemented with stipends by the partnering district. However, the funding received from the grant was initially reduced prior to being eliminated. While the issue of capacity is addressed in the final chapters, the commitment between the partners served as a catalyst to continue the project even with the limited resources.

The coaching of the individual principals entailing bi-monthly visits at their respective school-sites required the university facilitator to allocate four days per month, in an effort to facilitate bi-monthly Administrators' PLCs and conduct the individual site-based visitations. The university facilitator did not have the capacity to continue this effort without additional monetary resources, and without additional support from university colleagues.

The Administrators' PLC has commenced its fourth year. Unfortunately, the coaching component of the model had to be terminated, due to issues of capacity. Even though the coaching component was terminated two years ago, several of the principals continue to ask for this support. It was even suggested that perhaps they could receive a site-visitation on a monthly basis, if bi-monthly visitations are not feasible. While issues of capacity are addressed in the final chapters, the principals' request to continue a form of this component has implications for the pK-20 pipeline.

RECOMMENDATIONS FOR SUSTAINING THE ADMINISTRATORS' PLC MODEL

Systems are fluid, complex, and not immune to outside factors, as highlighted with the capacity issues that led to the removal of the coaching component. While the stakeholders have forged a strong university partnership bound together by a cultivated shared purpose, it is inconceivable to believe that this interdependent relationship will continue indefinitely. Therefore, continuous exploration of how the model can be modified to sustain the improvements made within the district is imperative. Multifaceted types of data to include improved test-score data, climate data, self-assessment data as well as data collected reflecting principals' changed behaviors, has been collected and analyzed throughout this project, providing indicators of principals changed behaviors as it correlates to instructional practices.

From the lens of the university facilitator, it is the hope that the district can sustain a variation of the model that embeds the principles of the conceptual framework, after the formal closure of the university's participation and support.

Variations of the model could involve the following possibilities:

- The non-negotiable aspect should entail a commitment to continuous PLCs for Administrators, where the focus is on their individual and collective learning, as it correlates to improving learning and teaching outcomes.

    Based on the experience of the 5-year project, the recommendation made to the superintendent and associate superintendent is that at a minimum, bi-monthly Administrators' PLCs are held. It has been observed that when the members of the Administrators' PLC meet less than twice a month, the members have increased difficulty in regrouping, maintaining a collective focus, and working together cohesively. It is important to note that the recommendation to decrease the role of the university facilitator for the purpose of increasing internal capacity has not been fully met. The observed factors and potential barriers are addressed further in the final chapters.
- As the transition is made to holding Administrators' PLCs without university involvement, the university facilitator facilitates one PLC each month, and the alternate PLC is facilitated by one of the principals or central office administrators. The goal of this approach is designed to build internal capacity, while receiving support from the university facilitator. Implementing this recommendation provides continuous opportunities for another member of the PLC outside of the university facilitator the task of asking poignant questions, preparing a written summary, synthesizing the learning of the PLC, and preparing an agenda to the members, which guides the work and expectations for the forthcoming PLC. We have experimented with this recommendation, with limited degrees of success. These dynamics and factors are also addressed in the final chapters.
- The individualized coaching sessions with the principals can be provided bi-monthly or monthly, or on an as needed basis, determined by differentiated need, as it aligns to meeting the outcomes put forth by the Administrators' PLC and district outcomes. As indicated earlier, this recommendation is contingent upon internal and external funding resources, and the selection of a coach or coaching team that can provide support in alignment to the district mission and purpose, while meeting the specific needs of the principals at the respective sites.

DEVELOPING THE MODEL FOR THE ADMINISTRATORS' PLC

EXCERPTS, GOALS AND OUTCOMES OF THE ADMINISTRATORS' PLC

2009–2010: FIRST YEAR OF THE ADMINISTRATORS' PLC

During the first year of the Administrators' PLC, the focus was placed on providing a consistent platform that served to facilitate deep, focused, job-embedded conversations and activities designed to build upon principals' instructional capacity, for the goal of providing developmentally aligned assistance to their teachers, to affect increased student achievement.

During our early work, it was imperative to provide principals with frameworks and models embedded by research-based practices, which would serve to both ground and guide our work. The principals were introduced to the SREB 13 Critical Success Factors (SREB, 2008). While all 13 critical success factors were important, it was equally important for principals to establish a focus, and make assessments based on what was perceived to be the areas of most need, which would serve to also increase buy-in to the process, risk0taking and ownership. Implementing the principles of shared-decision making, the principals, associate superintendent, and superintendent selected three critical factors, one from each Competency. The shared consensus between the stakeholders served to establish a focus and ground the work for the 2009–2010 academic school year.

- Competency 1: *Effective principals have a comprehensive understanding of school and classroom practices that contribute to student achievement.*
  - CSF 1 **focusing on student achievement:** creating a focused mission to improve student achievement and a vision of the elements of schools, curriculum and instructional practices that make higher achievement possible.
- Competency 2: *Effective principals have the ability to work with teachers and others to design and implement continuous student improvement.*
  - CSF 4 **creating a caring environment:** *developing a school organization where faculty and staff understand that every student counts and where every student has the support of a caring adult.*
- Competency 3: *Effective principals have the ability to provide the necessary support for staff to carry out sound school, curriculum and instructional practices.*
  - CSF 8 **initiating and managing change:** *understanding the change process and using leadership and facilitation skills to manage it effectively.*

WIGGINS AND MCTIGHE MODEL OF UNDERSTANDING BY DESIGN (1998)

The principals were introduced to a conceptual framework which entails two significant elements: The "backwards design" instructional design model, and the "Six Facets of Understanding." The model of backward design is centered on the concept that the design process should first begin with identifying the desired results and then "work backwards" to develop instruction, as opposed to the traditional approach guided by the topics to be covered (Wiggins & McTighe, 1998).

It was determined that the principals needed to understand and integrate this conceptual framework in an effort to structure and align our activities and efforts to our agreed upon outcomes. Another rationale for introducing this model and subsequent models in context to our established outcomes, changing developmental needs, and activities, was to provide the principals with continuous opportunities to integrate theoretical frameworks and underpinnings with applicable practice. An underlying principle of the Administrators' PLC was to utilize the structure of this platform for continuous learning as it aligned to the outcomes, which involved the integration of theory into practice.

BOOK STUDIES

In adherence to the practice of integrating theory into contextual practice, book studies were introduced during the first year of the Administrators' PLC and comprised a significant component of our early work. The practice of selecting books that aligned to our outcomes and areas of foci was instrumental to building upon principal knowledge. It was observed that as the principals' perceptions of the relevance of the Administrators' PLC grew, their participation in the book studies increased. This involvement included increased decision-making as to which books should be selected, in addition to their facilitation of the book studies.

In subsequent sessions, reflective of the growth of the Administrators' PLC, principals began to provide specific examples of how they implemented components of the readings in their respective school sites, sharing practice with their colleagues and providing recommendations. Another observation that was made during the second and third years of the Administrators' PLC pertained to principals' changed conversations and how they perceived the changed priorities of their practice. The language used by the principals in context to the discussions echoed the specific language that was embedded in the educational literature. It was observed that the principals increasingly referred to themselves as instructional leaders, making multiple connections between their role and their charge to build teacher capacity. It became increasingly common to hear them use phrases like: "We need to have evidence that this practice supports our outcomes." "We must challenge assumptions that do not support our mission, and practices that are not best for students." The question, are "We really being student-centered?" was heard with increased frequency when disconnected practices were addressed.

The principals' sense of urgency to change the culture in their respective school-sites and to affect student achievement was piqued. However, it is important not to underestimate the complexity of this process, the time and commitment involved in building individual and collective leadership capacity, as well as the implications this change had for the partnership's commitment to our continued growth as stakeholders representing the university and district. It is important to assert that these changes in the principals were not observed with consistency until the second

DEVELOPING THE MODEL FOR THE ADMINISTRATORS' PLC

year of the Administrators' PLC, which was during the third year of the university-district partnership.

As the facilitator representing the university, I was abreast on educational literature and its applicability to building leadership capacity and to continuous school improvement. However, I need to remain intentional on engaging in professional development that affected the changing context of the district. Therefore, I made a concerted effort as learner, to attend many of their on-going trainings. These trainings were often connected to the mandated and internal initiatives implemented, which included PD 360°, Literacy training that aligned to the District Educational Plan for Student Success (EPSS) plan, Response to Intervention (RtI), Professional Learning Communities, and most recently, training on new technology involving walkthroughs conducted on I-pads: "MyWaltkthroughTool," and The Common Core Standards.

I learned that my effectiveness as a facilitator had bearing to the level of relevancy that the principals perceived me to have. My ability to integrate the application of the educational literature on best practices in context to the programmatic and systematic initiatives that comprised the principals' reality was a critical tenet to maintaining the effectiveness of the Administrators' PLC. As the processes and activities of each year of the Administrators' PLC are highlighted, excerpts of the book studies are provided in context to the session and to the year.

THREE ESTABLISHED OUTCOMES IN 2009

1. Increase capacity of principals as instructional leaders as it connects to building teacher capacity of teachers through engaging in the following activities:
   a. Readings of best practices as determined by the members of the PLC
   b. Readings during the early sessions included: *What Works in Schools* (Marzano, 2006); *Leading Professional Learning Communities* (Hord & Sommers, 2008); *The Art & Science of Teaching* (Marzano, 2007).
   c. Engaging as a group in PD 360°, which required the watching of the video clips as a group and addressing best practices that were modeled
   d. Conducting individual walk-throughs on a regular basis and also as a group. The observations of the walk-throughs served to facilitate discussion on reflective practice.

2. Principals were provided with consistent opportunities to examine and practice how to developmentally move a teacher to the next level and increase efficacy in observing and modeling effective teaching practices for facilitating higher level thinking skills; providing continuous opportunities to help teachers create a teaching and learning environment that promotes reasoning, generates meaningful discussion, extends upon students' responses, and helps students to make meaningful connections in context to learning in the classroom. An intended

outcome was that principals will demonstrate increased evidence to engage in meaningful and reflective practice with their respective teachers.
3. A third outcome that was intended to guide our work during the first year of the Administrators' PLC, was centered on observed indicators of collegial learning and interaction, increased risk-taking, ownership for one's learning, cohesiveness and trust amongst the members of the learning community.

SUMMARY OF A SESSION TOWARD THE END OF THE 2009–2010 ACADEMIC SCHOOL YEAR

"During our last PLC, the conversation was centered on student learning and instruction, where strategic ideas for providing continuous support for teachers was evident."

- Poignant questions that led to further discussion were raised after reading and discussing book chapters 2 and 3 from *Leading Professional Learning Communities*. Chapter 2 addressed and focused on the question, "Why Leadership?" as it connects to learning communities. Chapter 5 addressed the skills needed for effectively leading professional learning communities that have the potential of making a difference on the teaching behaviors that can have a positive effect on student achievement.
- The chapters selected in the book studies served as a springboard for extended discussion, bringing to light topics and/or strategies that are relevant to the readings.
  - Extended core time for Tier II (RtI) to lengthen learning time above and beyond the core was raised by one of the principal participants
- It was agreed upon that principals would bring a component form the PD 360° training in an effort to continue our conversations centered on instruction. This would also provide opportunities in context for principals to share expertise and practice.
- One of the principal participants reinforced the integral components necessary for professional development to be effective with teachers and principals: The professional development needs to be:
  - On-going;
  - Job-embedded;
  - Result-driven
- Principals brought to light that for future district-wide professional development trainings, the principals need the PD to be integrated with the "talking heads." Therefore,
  - Opportunities for practice must be embedded within the context of the PD;
  - Presenters also need to model the concepts

- An excellent discussion centered on the questions, "As your role as a principal, in what ways do you inspire teachers," and "How do you strive to make continuous learning meaningful?"

The following comments captured the thoughts in our session:

   - Principals helping teachers reflect on their own practice
   - Create meaningful opportunities
   - Guidance by principals to improve instruction
   - Consistently learning to empower our teachers and address areas that are meaningful to them
   - Self-reflection—asking ourselves, "Do staff members have a clear vision on how to improve students' learning?"
   - Leaders need to have knowledge for conducting impromptu meetings
   - Understand the personality of the teacher you are working with
   - Create and foster culture—rather than order people to be "cohesive"
   - Do not rush into an answer that prompts premature closure
   - Non-negotiable tenet: *Trust* must be embedded into the culture
   - "What actions are you implementing or practicing that promote learning?"
   - Inspiration is the key
   - "The best thing a principal can do is to create a culture or environment that supports teachers and learning."

- Principals were asked to reflect on questions from pp. 42–43 in *Leading Professional Learning Communities* (Hord & Sommers, 2008), which facilitated this and subsequent discussions. Examples of questions from the book study included:

   - How am I modeling learning?
   - How does the staff know that learning is our most important product?
   - Do staff and students see me learning? Do they hear me talking about learning?
   - How do you rate yourself as a learner? How would the staff and students rate you as a learner?
   - How am I helping to create a professional learning community in my school? In my district?
   - How much of my time is spent talking about and actively engaging in learning during my daily professional life?
   - How am I creating ongoing, job-embedded, results-driven professional learning for staff?
   - How do I get feedback from students about what makes learning more effective?
   - Do the district meetings I attend make sure part of the agenda includes learning discussion that would support learning communities?

A principal participant asked the other members of the group, "Where do you think we are now in comparison to where we were last year?" Another participant responded, "light years ahead."

CHAPTER 3

The Rationale of the Administrators' PLC

"Our work serves to model and provide aligned support for principals in context to their practice for the overarching purpose of supporting teacher development that connects to student achievement. A purposeful outcome of our work is for our leaders to be intentional with helping teachers become increasingly connected with teaching and learning." (Ludeke, 2010).

END OF YEAR PROGRESS FOR THE 2009–2010 ACADEMIC SCHOOL YEAR

- The Administrators' PLC was centered on deep conversations, analyses, and reflections incorporating best practices
- Learning from Book Studies were embedded into reflective discussion and practice
    - Focus on increasing principals' ability to maximize resources and existing school structures
    - PD 360°; books on best practices; a focus centered on leading effective professional learning communities; conducting effective classroom walkthroughs
- Engaged in assessing teachers' strengths
    - Principals engaged in meaningful conversations with teachers for promoting teacher development, specifically as it aligned to the goals and objectives of the Educational Plan for Student Success (EPSS).

GOALS AND OUTCOMES FOR 2010–2011

- To build upon the goals established during the 2009–2010 school year
- Concerted focus on providing evidence of application: putting learning into practice
- Provide opportunities for principals to facilitate the Administrators' PLC
- Reflect upon and assess practice at respective school sites as it connects to intended outcomes
- Provide sustained time in the form of individualized coaching to each principal at their respective school-sites; addressing issues of implementation, aligning the coaching with principals' individual needs and varying stages of development

2010–2011

EXCERPTS FROM SESSION SUMMARIES DURING THE SECOND SEMESTER OF THE 2010–2011 ACADEMIC SCHOOL YEAR

Recently, I was reviewing our goals for 2010–2011, and comparing these goals to our goals established during the 2009–2010 school year. I am pleased to share with each of you that the conversations and activities that are brought to light in our Administrators' PLC and also in our individual coaching sessions, align with the competencies selected from the SREB 13 Critical Success Factors (SREB, 2008) for what "principals need to know and be able to do."

The theme of our continued work is to share evidence of implementation as it pertains to our respective school sites.

EXAMPLES OF IMPLEMENTATION

Principal Natalia has implemented the agenda and summaries for PLCs at her school, and modeling the use of agendas and summaries. The goal for one of the members of each PLC is to complete a summary and agenda used for facilitating the PLC." Pertaining to the topic of facilitating an effective PLC, Principal Natalia reflected, "Many teachers do not see the value of a PLC, and will not see the value until they have attained efficacy and meaning of the process." She continued by saying, "This is systemic, new and uncomfortable for many veteran teachers." Principal Alecia is working on reflective and shared practice with her teachers in their PLCs. In conversation with one of her teachers, Principal Alecia asked, "Did you have an opportunity to observe each other in your respective classrooms? The teacher responded, "It's like you are the teacher and we are the students engaged in cooperative learning."

- The PLC definition which was completed in our PLC has been shared at several sites with teachers. Please continue to refine the working definition and bring back to our group so we can finalize the process.

HIGHLIGHTS FROM OUR BOOK STUDY AND RELATED CONVERSATIONS

The book used to guide our work at this juncture was, *Building a Professional Learning Community at Work: A Guide to the First Year* (Graham & Ferriter, 2010). For this specific session, we addressed Chapter 4: Supporting Team Development.

Principal Alecia shared the need for continuous reflection and assessment. "One of the areas that facilitate failure is the lack of focus. "This chapter examined the historical culture and PLCs can change the culture." This principal also addresses the tenets inherent to second-order change. "The days of isolated practice are over. Leaders must address the feelings of loss that occurs when second-order change is made." Principal Edward addressed the issue of impact. "While PLCs meet frequently, they need additional evidence that the conversations are yielding impact." Principal Edward also addressed the feelings of frustration. "Frustration can be an indicator that that the PLC is moving teachers out of their comfort zones. If you are not feeling frustration, you are probably not accomplishing anything." Another principal summarized the discussion by expressing, "As administrators, we have embraced this process."

CHAPTER 3

STAGES OF PLCS—CHAPTER 4, P.70

- The stages of PLCs were addressed, which can be referenced on p. 70. The stages are: *Forming, Storming, Norming, and Performing.* "It is important for principals to be able to determine at which developmental level their PLCs are at, and be able to provide assistance and support in guiding their teachers within each PLC to the next stage."
- Questioning prompts reflective of each stage of "Bloom's Taxonomy" were modeled during the last PLC. "This certainly has implications for principals as they observe teaching and also as they observe and participate in PLCs. The groups can practice having focused conversations on what teaching and learning may look like when higher levels of questioning occurs." "This also has potential implications for lesson planning, differentiated instructional strategies, and for self-reflection. Teachers can reflect on specific strengths, and areas of supports needed as they learn to embrace the continuous learning process." "These conversations and practices will not occur over night, but the knowledge we are acquiring can be systematically incorporated and monitored in the PLCs, as it corresponds to the developmental stage of each PLC."

NEXT STEPS

For the forthcoming session, please provide evidence of having facilitated one of your PLCs to focus on *implementation.*

➢ Principals, please come prepared to share your assessment of:

  o What stages your PLCs are at;
  o Address evidence that supports your assessment;
  o Share strategies and next steps you might implement in an effort to facilitate the movement of a PLC from one stage to the next.

➢ As a recommendation, have your teachers bring the resource guide provided, *Master Instructional Strategies* (Lujan, Collins, & Love, 2008) with them to their respective PLCs. However, provide them with guidance in using this resource to facilitate a focused conversation centered on using instructional strategies in context to their work, which may guide their next steps.

PRINCIPALS' PERCEPTIONS OF THE CONTINUOUS IMPROVEMENT PROCESS

The overarching theme of the Administrators' PLC held in early spring, involved a deep discussion centered on the purpose of a PLC, and what it takes to implement and sustain meaningful PLCs which: "correspond to building teacher capacities in an environment that supports shared and continuous learning, for the collective outcome of implementing student-centered practices affect student achievement."

The subsequent PLCs and decisions made for the remainder of the school year, served to expand upon and support this theme. The summary of this PLC session was focused on principals' perceptions of the continuous improvement process, and the impact the Administrators' PLC may had on changing teacher practice. Armando, the Director of Special Education Services commented, "From my perspective as the Special Education Director, there is increased evidence of student-centered practices in our schools."

Principal Isidro indicated, "Teachers are increasingly looking at student outcomes, and that it would be difficult to implement a PLC at his school without the platform and work completed in our Administrators' PLC."

Principal Natalia shared her perspective regarding book studies. "I feel that the book studies have played an important role in my learning process and that we may not have read the books on our own or had the opportunity to discuss them with each other without this platform."

During this session, discussion was centered on how to embed the PLC into the day, and which models were the most conducive for accomplishing this task. The associate superintendent provided feedback regarding model selection. "PLCs and reflective practice has to be embedded into the day, and that there are a variety of models that are available for elementary, middle and high schools." He suggested that "the principals look at the multiple books written by DuFour, DuFour & Eaker, which have been distributed to the principals, in order to determine the best model suited for the respective sites."

The former District Superintendent emphatically stated in response to the discussion, is that "the goal that should be embedded is evidence of implementation."

The former superintendent, who had made a commitment to support and partake as a learner in the PLCs, made the following assertion as it pertained to the ongoing theme in our PLC:

> The learning curve in a school that is implementing PLCs is often a steep one. Therefore, it is imperative that the principals are able to provide evidence that teachers are sharing practice and research-based strategies, in addition to assessing where the teachers are, and determining next steps necessary for improving the effectiveness of the PLC.

> The former superintendent raised the poignant question to the group,

> To what extent have the principals had the opportunity for the teachers to develop a lesson within the PLC?

Throughout this discussion, it was observed that the associate superintendent continued to thread the research-based strategy coined by DuFour, DuFour, and Eaker. (2008) and DuFour, DuFour, Eaker, and Karhanek (2010) of *"tight and loose."* This phrase was translated as the non-negotiable and negotiable tenets and practices necessary for guiding the continuous improvement process.

During another PLC focused on the themes of continuous improvement and impact, as it corresponds to the role of the principal, the former district superintendent posed this question to the group: "What do principals need to know and do as it pertains to your role in your PLC?"

CHAPTER 3

This question, which has been previously addressed in the group as it comprised the SREB framework that continues to guide our continuous improvement process, generated a series of responses. The discussion facilitated the final question, which served to guide forthcoming PLCs. The former superintendent asked, "As principals, how much of your time is centered on instructional conversations?"

The responses to the question raised by the superintendent varied from 10% to 30%. The superintendent emphatically referenced the research on best practices in his response:

> According to the research regarding instructional conversations as it connects to student achievement, principals need to spend 65% of their time engaged in meaningful instructional conversations with their teachers.

The superintendent asked each principal to self-reflect on how time on instructional conversations with teachers will increase. In adherence to the theme of continuous improvement, evidence of impact and the role of the leader, it was clear that the former superintendent was holding the principals accountable for the school improvement process.

The above summary of this session was the last session prior to the principals' attendance in "The Professional Learning Communities at Work Institute." The participation of the principals and the rationale for sending the principals to the institute after they have had the opportunity to partake as members of their own PLC is addressed. As we prepared for our participation in the institute and adjourned our PLC for 2010–2011 school year, I posed a reflective question to the group:

> Based on our individual and collective growth as principals and administrators, what specific skills, attributes, and dispositions do we need to continue to develop during the 2011–2012 academic school year? What do we need our schools to look like or move closer to, during the forthcoming year?

2011–2012

ONE OF THE MOST SIGNIFICANT TOOLS available to a school that is attempting to build a PLC is this process of clarifying essential outcomes, building common assessments, reaching consensus on the criteria by which teachers will judge the quality of student work, and working together to analyze data and improve results.

On Common Ground

The 2011–2012 Administrators' PLC was commenced by the following communication I had prepared for the members of the PLC in an effort to synthesize work from previous years, and establish a tighter focus with increased evidence of implementation and impact for the 2011–2012 school year. From my assessment, based on our numerous strengths, providing evidence of sustained implementation of leadership practices that connected to a critical mass of changed teachers' behaviors was still a weaker link, proving to be a multi-year effort.

SEPTEMBER 2011

"I have been analyzing the data and synthesizing summaries for our Administrators' PLC for three years! We have just embarked on our fourth year as a professional learning community."

Since I consistently incorporate the four-step framework that pertains to data, I examine our PLC from that lens. In the analyses of the data collected at the end of our sessions, I asked,

1. What does the data tell us?
2. What is it not telling us, or what more do we need to know?
3. What is there to celebrate?
4. And what are the next steps to guide the continuous improvement process? (Holcomb, 2004)

I am pleased to share with our team that the data reveals much in the way of *celebration*. In synthesizing the conversations, there is consistent evidence that we have individually and collectively internalized the process and tenets that adhere to the literature we have been reading. As an increasingly cohesive and reflective group, we share practice to assist one another, ask critical questions in context, use data to substantiate our decisions, and have increased levels of urgency to build upon teacher capacity, both individually and within the PLCs at our respective sites; as it connects to attaining a system that produces high levels of student achievement.

The following quotes that I captured in our sessions serve as one form of evidence to substantiate the above findings.

"We have a common theme–a collective vision," which will make it more difficult to put one system against the other." Director of Special Education, Armando

"We are providing evidence of how our administrative culture and interdependent culture fosters continuous learning." Principal Natalia

"I have worked in many districts and this is the first time I have felt the warmth and the feeling that I am not alone." Principal Leticia

"We need to have intrinsic motivation as it corresponds to sustainable change." Principal Edward

"Formative and summative assessments have to substantiate how they are achieving the target areas." Principal Elisa

"We develop work plans that serve as a mechanism to bridge the gap between the PDP and growth plan." Principal Tiffany

"We have talked about what continuous mentoring for each other looks like, and will be able to support one another." Associate Superintendent

Since our participation in the "Learning Communities at Work" Conference in the summer, we have met three times in an effort to establish a shared consensus

CHAPTER 3

of what our priorities are for this year, which will become our focus. Each time we have met, we have engaged in varying activities which were *not* completed. However, there is a general consensus that we need to continue to focus our efforts on *implementation,* to ensure that our Administrators' PLC maintains its relevancy and provides specific evidence that we have increased our efficacy to meeting the diverse needs of our students and teachers.

During our last session, the focus on application and implementation was more clearly defined. There was a general consensus that we as a team need to focus on "providing concrete support to teachers and specific next steps for improving their instructional practices." In analyzing what the data is *not telling us*, or what I can infer from this process "this year we have developed to the level and possess the varied attributes and skill sets to really drill down on this specific task, and be able to ask what specific activities and practice we need in order to arrive at this outcome." Second, we need to focus on how we will measure that we are getting closer to arriving at this goal. In other words, using DuFour, DuFour, and Eaker's (2008) question "How will we know when we get there?"

Since a non-negotiable tenet of a PLC includes arriving at a shared consensus using data, I have provided my analyses and recommendations, continuing to utilize this four-step framework. As a team, we demonstrate increasing commitment to utilizing the platform of a PLC both in our setting as well at our respective school sites to create a collegial culture that can build teacher capacity and incorporate systemic interventions for our students. Our consistent book studies has served as an integral part of this on-going journey, as we cannot practice as instructional leaders without the ability to integrate research-based practices into applicable context.

"We do **not** have sufficient evidence that we are incorporating and assessing everything we are reading as it applies to our specific focus for this year."

Incorporating the principles of the Wiggins and McTighe Model (1998), a model we have become familiar with, we need to ensure that as a team, we are in agreement about our *outcome.* Then, planning backwards, we must ensure that what we learn, *we apply, and that the application aligns* to the shared outcome. Embracing this process will also help to avoid the temptation of "covering curriculum and not creating curriculum." Based on the collected data and the process that I have described, I am recommending that the next steps necessary for meeting our shared outcome involve the reading and application of two books. As we continue the practice of book study, we want to integrate the specific steps that are proposed in the readings, as they specifically "apply to assessing an actual administrator-teacher conversation centered on improving that teacher's practice."

I have taken the time to read the book *Advancing Formative Assessment in Every Classroom, A Guide for Instructional Leaders* (Moss & Brookhart, 2009). Reading this timely book gave me more reason for us to celebrate our successes. The tenets in this book reinforce that we have attained the knowledge, attributes and skill-sets to *apply* the specific strategies in context to "concretely help our teachers improve upon their instructional practices, which is the cornerstone of a PLC." Helping ourselves become more proficient in helping teachers is also paramount to this process. Reading this book also provided specific and concrete strategies that we can use to help us assess and guide teaching practice, but also to provide tools for teachers to do the same with their students in their classrooms and for their students in their PLCs.

In summary, I am recommending that we incorporate the Wiggins and McTighe Model of Backward Planning to ensure that we align our activities to our outcome, and then put in *criteria to measure* that we are meeting our goals. To the extent that we can do this, we accomplish two overarching principles deeply embedded in the work of PLCs. We are authentically engaging in a continuous learning process, and using data to guide our work and make adjustments as it corresponds to our outcome, hopefully built by a shared consensus. Paraphrasing the work of DuFour et al and colleagues (2006, 2008,. 2010) "We determine what we want to look like, and put in mechanisms to help us know that we are getting there!"

PLCs are a journey and they are not easy. What we have done and continue to do, are unprecedented. While the phrase PLC is liberally used throughout this state, I have not observed a model that parallels a fluid, complex organizational system where we come together as a partnership over the years to further our purpose. Having said this, I have this sense of urgency to provide concrete evidence that we are meeting our shared outcome for the 2011–2012 academic school year.

2012–2013

This session reflected our second session of the 2012–2013 academic school year. Upon reflection of the outcome of this session, it was necessary to review the goals and outcomes of our work to date, regroup, and provide recommendations that can guide this forthcoming year.

Taking time to re-read and synthesize the summaries and agendas, and data reflecting our multi-year efforts, I am pleased to share the several authentic strengths indicated by the data. These findings suggest that the members in the Administrators' PLC:

- place an increased focus on instructional practices
- value their respective roles as instructional leaders
- have improved their ability to question teachers and have focused conversations centered on student-centered learning practices in the classroom
- increasingly view their role as building the capacity of teachers
- increased emphasis on accountability and aligned practices
- value continuous learning
- value shared practice
- and generally feel more competent in addressing the complex change process within their respective PLCs as building principals

Since our process embeds first and second-order change principles, the data also reveals areas that imply need for continuous improvement.

CHAPTER 3

The findings indicate:

- need for increased focus and streamlined focus
- need for increased evidence of follow-through on implementation
- need for increased consistency with practices
- evidence of impact on implementation as it corresponds to goals and outcomes

Synthesis and Implications of the findings

In analyzing the findings, it is encouraging that the findings suggest that as individual stakeholders comprising the Administrators' PLC, our values and beliefs have facilitated a collectively shared vision which drives our work. The findings also suggest that most of the members in the Administrators' PLC have internalized the process, and have made a paradigm shift in thinking and in practice throughout the years of this deep work. These are critical attributes of second-order change; the most difficult to accomplish.

Implications for our continuous improvement fall more closely in the category of first-order change. This includes the need for increased skill building and efficacy in specific areas, a need to plan backwards as it corresponds to outcome, and *increase the impact* of our individual and collective efforts. This will entail that we collect evidence that what we implement "aligns with our decided upon goals and outcomes, and that we have evidence that it has made an impact on student achievement."

RECOMMENDATIONS

For our next Administrators' PLC, I would like us to collectively agree upon an outcome, the tools we will use to accomplish that outcome, and the evidence we will collect, to determine the impact of our efforts on student-achievement. For example: Our outcome and focus in our Administrators' PLC can be centered on: Increasing Teacher Practice based on selecting two or three components from the Teacher Competencies. Our initial steps would be to ask ourselves specifically, "What would increased teacher practice look like?" and "How will we help our teachers get there (Using the competencies to guide the question)? We would then agree upon "What evidence would need to be collected that would measure impact?" In other words, "How would we know that we attained our goals and met the outcome?"

Planning backwards (incorporating Wiggins & McTighe model of backward designing) by starting with the outcome in mind, helps us to maintain a *streamlined focus, aligning* our efforts and tools implemented for attaining the outcome. An example of a **tool** would be implementing walk-throughs with fidelity, increasing our capacity of providing meaningful feedback to the teachers, and having in-depth instructional conversations that increase the focus on teacher development. These practices have implications for increasing our ability to collect formative data, which if responded to with fidelity, will have a bearing on the summative aspects of evaluations. However, as we have all learned through this process over the years, focusing on development which requires increased visibility in the classrooms and continuous informal and formal instructional conversations is a non-negotiable attribute of *collegial schools*.

Maintaining a tight focus on the agreed upon outcome, will have implications for our professional development needs that will arise as we address this outcome at our respective school sites as well as in our Administrators' PLC. It will also have implications on the mechanisms in place in the district and in our respective school sites. Borrowing the phrase from DuFour, DuFour, and Eaker (2008; DuFour, DuFour, Eaker, & Karhanek, 2010) of "tight and loose," "We must be tight on the outcome, but can be "loose" or more flexible as to what our needs may look like," taking into consideration the unique aspects and differences in our schools.

Please read this summary and the implications of the findings in its entirety. The focus of the forthcoming session will be to define and commit to a collectively agreed upon outcome that will define our work and our professional growth for the 2012–2013 school year. I feel privileged to have embarked on our fifth year of this collaboration, centered on our innovative work.

PROFESSIONAL LEARNING COMMUNITIES AT WORK SUMMIT

Towards the close of the second year of the Administrators' PLC, a collective decision between central office leaders was made to invest in sending the principals and teachers representing each school site to the "Professional Learning Communities at Work Summit." There was a shared consensus between the members of the university-district partnership, that implementing this step after the principals have had an opportunity to partake in a PLC, engage in the readings and have opportunities for shared practice within the structure of the PLC, would increase the effectiveness of the principals' ability to implement the practices with their teachers at their respective school-sites.

As indicated in my summaries shared with each member in the Administrators' PLC, the data collected revealed that they had embraced and internalized the principles inherent to an effective PLC. However, consistent implementation and evidence of impact as it connects to changing teachers' behaviors and practice that have positive outcomes for student-achievement, has proven to be the weakest-link in this otherwise successful multi-year effort.

A caution regarding this assessment, which has continuous improvement implications for our Administrators' PLC, relates to sending the principals prior to our sustained work in building leadership capacity, as it may have proven to be less than viable for the district. As a former principal who has implemented the DuFour Model of PLCs as a reform initiative over a decade ago, I continue to be a proponent of this model for facilitating deep cultural shifts in schools. However, as reinforced in the literature in Chapters 1 and 2 of this book, the effectiveness of this model is largely incumbent on the skills and vision of the school principal.

CHAPTER 3

Over the years, I have had the opportunity to attend several institutes and trainings on this model. I make the following observation: Most of the conferences are quite large, comprising mostly teacher participants. During my attendance in the last institute, an "ice-breaker" was implemented. Participants were asked to raise their hands as it corresponded to their respective positions. When asked, "How many of you in the audience are teachers?" over 90% of the participants raised their hand. When asked, "How many of you in this room are principals or assistant principals," a handful of participants raised their hand; most of those who raised their hands represented our rural district. When asked, "How many of you in this room are superintendents or are from central office?" Three hands were raised. One of those hands belonged to the associate superintendent, who comprises the university-district partnership. When asked, "How many of you in this room are board members?" one hand was raised. Finally, the question was posed to higher-ed. "How many of you in this room represent a higher-education institution?" My hand was the only hand in the air, out of nearly two thousand participants.

Engaging in this moving activity served to reinforce a longstanding premise. A model designed to facilitate deep organizational change within the context of schooling, has an absence of the leaders who represent the pK-20 pipeline. Over the years of attending conferences like these, I am always pleased to see the overwhelming participation of teachers. However, the absence of the stakeholders who have the power to support, implement and sustain these complex models has implications for the pK-20 pipeline, and systemic continuous improvement. Questions that come to mind include: "Are the underpinnings of this model and similar models designed to bring about systems-change really understood?" What are possible next steps that could make the complexity of this model and the implications for facilitating deep change more readily known? To what extent do the districts and school board members understand that this is not a program that is purchased, rather a whole-systems approach designed to facilitate school improvement efforts that can have an impact on student achievement? What systems of support need to be put into place for higher-education to take an active role in increasing the effectiveness of implementing and sustaining initiatives that heavily impact the teachers and school leaders whom we prepare? "To what extent will the impetus for these models in an era of continuous accountability and continuous improvement have an impact on how university-district partnerships are conceptualized?" The answers to these questions are complex and not readily answered. However, the findings in this book have implications for contributing to the research that can expound upon these questions and others that have not been brought to the forefront.

CONCLUSION

This chapter described in-depth the processes that facilitated the emergence and development of an Administrators' PLC. This platform designed to provide sustained professional development, focused on building the leadership capacity within the district, as well as providing continuous learning opportunities for all stakeholders participating in the Administrators' PLC. This chapter connected the processes implemented to the overarching purpose of the Administrators' PLC. A discussion and rationale for the activities and decisions made throughout the progression of this multi-year project, leading to continuous improvement efforts, was delineated.

Chapter 4 formally introduces the principals and the context in which they work. The voices of the principals were briefly introduced in Chapter 3, in context to their participation in the Administrators' PLC that has spanned four consecutive years. Chapter 4 shares the insights and perceptions pertaining to critical dimensions centered on the comprehensive role of the Principalship. The principals discussed how they were prepared as principals, reflecting on their respective principal preparation programs, which influenced how they perceived their role as principal prior to their participation in the Administrators' PLC. These principals also provided reflective descriptions of their early professional development experiences once they became seated principals.

CHAPTER 4

INSIGHTS ON THE PRINCIPALS PRIOR TO THE PLC

Chapter 3 provided an in-depth description of the processes that facilitated the emergence, development, and progression of the Administrators' PLC. The principals' voices were embedded into context to their participation in the Administrators' PLC, which was highlighted in the Administrators' PLC summaries, spanning a 4-year timeframe.

Chapter 3 introduced the principals and administrators who participated in this project. The focus of Chapter 4 and the forthcoming chapters centered on findings and implications are placed on further understanding how these principals made contextual meaning of their learning throughout the process of their sustained professional development. These findings attempted to fully describe the sequences (Rowlands, 2005) of the principals' individual and collective learning, which have bearing on the conditions that determine innovation processes and theory building (Rowlands, 2005).

SETTING AND HISTORICAL CONTEXT OF THE SCHOOL DISTRICT

The rural school district, fictitiously given the name of the Southwest School District, commenced its early work with the Alliance at the university, prior to the development of the university-district partnership. Historically, the Southwest School District is a mining area, located in the Southwest region of the United States, approximately 70 miles from the Mexican border. The Southwest School District is comprised of three villages, with respective approximate populations of 2,600; 2,000; and 1,500 residents. The district also serves students who reside in small and separated rural communities varying from approximately 100 to 600 residents, as reported in the 2000 census. As part of the historical backdrop, it is important to draw attention to the fact that students and families living in these communities have deep roots that date back several generations.

THE PARTICIPANTS

The participants in the project comprised 7 seated principals, 6 who are currently seated as principals. The additional participants in the project included: the director of instruction who served as a former elementary principal in the district; two former elementary principals; one former middle-school principal who is now retired; one former superintendent; a current interim superintendent; the associate superintendent who serves as the district partner; a director of special education

CHAPTER 4

services; a secondary assistant principal; and the researcher who continues to serve as the primary facilitator of the Administrators' PLC. The participant demographics of current and former participants comprised: three Caucasian males; two Caucasian females; five Hispanic females; and three Hispanic males. In an effort to maintain the confidentiality of the participants, the principal participants are introduced as Edward, Natalia, Isidro, Tiffany, Kurt, Elisa, Leticia, and Alecia. The Director of Special Education is introduced as Armando. Savannah, a former elementary principal at the district, now serves in the capacity of Director of Instruction. The Superintendent, Associate Superintendent, and the writer who served as the university facilitator, are referred to by their titles. This is done in an effort to maintain distinction between the participants and the partners between the university and school district, who also served as participants in the Administrators' PLC.

The principal participants disclosed critical insights centered on how they were prepared as principals, reflecting on their respective principal preparation programs. Their experiences influenced how they perceived their role as principal prior to their participation in the Administrators' PLC. These principals also provided reflective descriptions of their early professional development experiences once they became seated principals.

INTERPRETIVE CASE STUDY APPROACH

Embedded in the discussions are excerpts from the emergent themes from the descriptive data, which were analyzed using qualitative methods in adherence to the interpretative case study approach (Merriam, 1998). The author was vested in gleaning a deep understanding of the learning processes and the ways that principals made meaning of their learning experiences in a sustained professional development setting, which could lead to building upon theory (Merriam, 1998). The choice to use an interpretative case study approach was influenced by the author's exploratory approach (Rowlands, 2005) centered on understanding the social context of how principals constructed their experiences and made meaning (Rowlands, 2005) from their individual and collective knowledge acquired throughout their shared job-embedded learning derived from the Administrators' PLC.

The perceptions of these participants prior to participating in the learning from the Administrators' PLC, guided the further exploration of the inquiry. The inquiry was centered on what principals perceived happens when they engage in a professional learning community model over a sustained period of time, that closely embodies similar skill-sets, dispositions and attributes that reflect the specific tenets of the whole-reform models they are charged to implement, as well as the leadership principles brought to light in the literature of what the 21st century principal needs to know and be able to do.

The author was specifically interested in understanding the lived and multiple realities constructed by the principals (Merriam, 1998) to guide and inform the study. Therefore, the focus was to facilitate an inductive approach for understanding the meaning of their individual and collective processes. Unveiling the "story behind the factors," (Rowlands, 2005) from the principals' lived experiences, has implications for building upon an emergent theory of an under-researched topic focused on the sustained professional development experiences of principals. It is the hope of the author that the learning and findings derived from the multi-year project can be applied to further research and influence practice and policy in the field.

INTEGRATING THE ANALYSES

Having participated in this work with the principal participants, from the lens of the university facilitator, I have integrated the analyses of the principals' perceptions which have resulted in part, from the ongoing professional development embedded in the Administrators' PLC. Excerpts from individual Administrator PLCs summaries have been incorporated in context to the analyses as it corresponded with the specific discussion. The purpose of integrating interpretive commentary (Merriam, 1998) and analyses was to provide the reader with the voices of the university-district partnership, as well as an added dimension of the content, activities, and discussions which guided our early and progressive work as an Administrators' PLC.

While the voices of the participants were initially heard in Chapter 3, as the processes of building and developing the Administrators' PLC were described in depth, excerpts of the Administrators' PLCs, individual interviews and foci groups, are embedded with interpretive commentary (Merriam, 1998) in the findings chapters, in context to the specific discussion.

INSIGHTS ON PRINCIPAL PREPARATION

The discussion that was centered on principal preparation, revealed a prevalent theme highlighting the transition from the emphasis on management to the role of the instructional leader. Principal Kurtis reflected on the transition from the role of principal as manager to the role of instructional leader, pointing out that this type of preparation was not offered in his program of study.

> There is this whole movement now towards data-driven decision making and collaborative learning with teachers and with principals. These kinds of things were not included in my coursework. Because they just weren't present, I don't think in school administration.

Principal Elisa as well, reflected on the early shift in preparation emphasis that was being evidenced in university principal preparation programs.

> At the time I was earning my administrative degree, there was a transition from being a management type of principal, to a principal who focuses on instruction—more of being able to go into the classroom as an instructional leader.

CHAPTER 4

Principal Natalia discussed the focus of her program in 2001, which placed an emphasis on instructional leadership. Reflecting on her Educational Leadership program, she felt that

> finding a balance between the focus on instructional leadership and the management part of it, which I felt was really helpful in being able to see what my role needed to be. I needed to become more of an instructional leader, having the management under control, so that I could be that leader within my school, for my teachers and students. So I was, I think, really lucky to have had the professor that I had, who was looking at that as the main role of a principal.

According to Principal Tiffany, Clinical Supervision was embedded into her Educational Leadership program.

> With the one professor, it was a lot of the clinical instruction; Clinical Supervision. There was a focus on the idea of coaching teachers up, versus, just whatever. So I felt there was a lot of instruction on that.

Isidro also reflected on one professor whom he felt had made an impact on his learning during his principal preparation program.

> You know, the only preparation that I received, mostly consisted of theory. We read the books, and we discussed the stuff, and then we had discussions which really helped. We shared different ideas and different events, or things that happened at the school with one another. But I felt that the class that helped me the most was the School Law course. We had a professor who brought in court cases, and he brought in real life examples. The professor brought guest speakers, other school administrators to talk to us. We then slowly began to tie the theories together in that class. I felt that this was the course that I benefited the most from, and I just loved it.

EMERGENT THEMES

From my early data collection and sustained work in the Administrators' PLC with the principals and central office participants, several ideas emerged that pertained to the theme of instructional leadership and the role of instructional leader. These early indicators had implications for guiding the activities, practices, and discussions, which included the curricular framework and book studies that were embedded into the Administrators' PLC, addressed in detail in Chapter 3.

The participants in the Administrators' PLC were responsive to the differentiated and changing needs, which were reflected in our sustained work. While a concerted effort was made to align our work to the collectively agreed upon outcomes, we engaged in a continuous practice of assessment and reflection. The content of our activities were focused, yet adjustable, as we were acutely aware of the need to accommodate external forces that spanned the scope of the Administrators' PLC framework. These factors included directives and initiatives that were received from central office, state, and at the national level.

The changing needs of the principals and all participants, reflected in their individual and collective development were also considered. During the third year of the Administrators' PLC, our work has become heavily centered on the Common Core initiatives. The shift in emphasis had two implications: The ability to shift our attention on the Common Core initiatives reflected the development of our principals, in addition to our collective ability to embrace a continuous and adaptive process of improvement, necessary for addressing external change forces.

ADJUSTING TO CHANGING NEEDS

As the needs of principal participants changed, collective decisions to remove structures or initiatives which were perceived useful were implemented. A decision was made to discontinue the services of a purchased program that was once perceived as instrumental for the principals' development. This process supported the literature of continuous assessment which facilitates the removal of duplicitous programs, policies, and structures that are no longer perceived as effective for supporting the collectively shared outcome (DuFour, DuFour, Eaker, & Many, 2006).

CULTIVATING COMMON GROUND

Several of the participants felt that being an instructional leader was an integral component of effective principalship. The principals' initial perceptions, possibly influenced by their respective preparation programs, made it easier to gain consensus from the group, centered on building participants' capacity as instructional leaders in our preliminary work in the Administrators' PLC. While several of the principals in our early work felt that building instructional leadership capacity of our seated principals was central to their role as principal, the term "instructional leader" was randomly used, without a comprehensive grasp of what it meant to be an instructional leader. It was felt that much variation existed in terms of how this definition translated into operational practice. In our early work, most of the principals were not making the connection between the interdependence which exists between confidence as an instructional leader and the ability to facilitate high-functioning PLCs at their respective school sites (DuFour & Marzano, 2011; Matthews & Crow, 2010; Sergiovanni, 2005).

BUILDING INSTRUCTIONAL CAPACITY

In the early work of the university-district partnership, most of our well-intended principals were delegating or managing the PLCs at their respective school sites, and were minimally involved in shared collective practice with their teachers. As the facilitator from the university, it was my unwavering assessment, that unless specific

CHAPTER 4

criteria were met, the district would not likely realize significant changes in teachers' overall practice that would have an impact on district-wide student achievement, specifically with sub-populations.

Achieving a cohesive operational definition of what it meant and looked like to perform as an instructional leader, specifically as it pertained to creating and sustaining high-functioning PLCs at the respective sites was imperative. In addition, the principals needed to build their capacity as instructional leaders, and understand the interdependent relationship between their role as an instructional leader, and their ability to facilitate high-functioning PLCs that provided evidence of shared practice, continuous learning, with the collectively shared outcome on teacher growth and student-centered practices. The process of developing an operational definition of a Professional Learning Community (PLC) that reflected the voices of central office, principals and teachers, was a multi-year effort. We began this process during the first-year of the Administrators' PLC. The finalized version which has been adopted by Central Office was finalized during the third year of the Administrators' PLC. The finalized definition is found in Chapter 3.

CRITICAL ELEMENTS OF A LEARNING COMMUNITY

Matthews, Williams, and Stewart (2007 in Matthews & Crow, 2010) identified 10 common cultural elements found in successful PLCs. Chapter 1 provided an in-depth description of these critical elements. An identified critical element which guided our work in the early formation of the Administrators' PLC, was the element centered on "principal leadership that is focused on student learning" (Matthews & Crow, 2010). The role of this type of principal in a PLC is perceived as someone who possesses the vision and ability to create conditions that foster continuous adult learning and improvement in an effort to ensure that students can achieve the level of skills and attributes necessary for their success.

INCONSISTENT PRINCIPAL PREPARATION EXPERIENCES

Another important piece of data which emerged from the principals' voices pertaining to their principal preparation programs is that the principal participants experienced one or two professors who made an impact on their preparation. However, this was not necessarily consistent with their respective program of study. This finding had implications for our work, as we collectively determined which learning gaps needed to be addressed in our Administrators' PLC, as it correlated to their current role as seated principals, charged with leading schools that had a designation of School in Need of Improvement (SINOI).

MENTORING AND INTERNSHIP EXPERIENCES

The principal participants reflected on critical topics pertaining to their internship, mentorship, professional support, and perceived gaps in their professional development once they became seated principals. Meeting the specific and differentiated needs of the principals to accommodate the rapidly changing role of the principalship continues to be an influential dynamic that informs our collective practice in the Administrators' PLC.

Edward, Kurtis, and Elisa reflected on the emphasis placed on management during their respective internships. Edward expressed his frustration:

> In my internship I found it to be a little frustrating, only because I dealt with one side of things. I really only experienced the discipline side of the job. I shadowed a counselor for a portion of the internship, but that was about it.

Kurtis had a similar experience in his internship as he shared:

> With the various administrators whom I shadowed, I experienced varying management styles. I shadowed elementary principals; I shadowed intermediate principals; middle school and high school principals. While their styles were a little different, they all focused on management of the school. The focus was on the day-in, day-out management. I really did not shadow principals whom we might refer to today as leadership—instructional leadership type principals.

Kurtis added:

> At that time during my internship experience, in the late 80s, very early 90s, when I was completing my program, the focus was on the "nuts and bolts" of being a school administrator.

While Elisa's coursework had placed an increasing emphasis on the role of the instructional leader, she experienced a disconnect between what she was taught in her coursework, and what she experienced during her principal internship.

> At the school where I was completing my internship, I shadowed a principal whose focus was primarily on school management. From that principal, I learned how to manage a school. He stressed the importance of schedules for teachers, students, and buses.

Elisa's internship principal played an instrumental role in modeling the operational aspects of the school. However, it was not overly evident that he was significant in expanding and building on the foundational courses in her preparation program, which reflected more closely the changing role of the principalship.

MISSING PIECE IN PROFESSIONAL DEVELOPMENT

There was a specific interest in learning specifically in what ways the professional development of the principal participants were supported once they became seated principals. The findings were gleaned from multiple sources which included: principal interviews, foci groups, and our individual and group work with the principals prior to and during the formal development of the Administrators' PLC. Our sustained work as a group, also served to provide continuous data which serves to inform our practice and decisions made within the framework of the Administrators' PLC.

Principals Sharon and Kurtis described their professional development once they were seated principals, to primarily be self-directed. Principal Sharon described her professional development:

> I would attend conventions or workshops geared for school administrators. I also attended school board retreats so that I could learn more of the law, more of the legal side of school administration. I also capitalized on opportunities to attend conventions or workshops that addressed leadership issues. I felt that the legal aspect was an area of weakness. Therefore, I took the initiative to seek out opportunities that were available.

Kurtis reflected on his self-directed professional development by bringing to light that no one guided his professional development, or required his continuous learning once he became a seated principal.

> To be really honest, my professional development throughout my career was self-directed and voluntary. No one told me that I had to attend any of the professional development that I selected throughout the years. For example, when I left the principalship to become a superintendent, before I returned as a principal, I had significant latitude as to what kind of professional development I would select. Looking back, I was able to select professional development that turned out to be beneficial down the road. I attended a week-long training on the Baldrige Method.

Principal Leticia reflected on her "self-learning," which supported the varied training and professional development she received once she became a seated principal.

> Once I became an administrator, I did receive quite a bit of training in my previous district, which included evaluating staff. I considered much of my training, prior to participating in the on-going Administrators' PLC, as "self-learning" and "trial and error." I had co-workers who were always willing to work together and share ideas. We would call each other, but I also felt isolated.

Principal Kurtis spoke to the isolation a seated principal felt:

Prior to participating in the Administrators' PLC, I felt that there was quite a bit of isolation. Everybody was on their own in their buildings.

FIRST YEAR AS AN ADMINISTRATORS' PLC

The consensus to address existing learning gaps, increase group cohesiveness, and build upon instructional capacity for our principals became a priority for the stakeholders. Reinhartz and Beach (2004) are an example of the many researchers who reinforce the concept that school leadership has become more important as it has been linked to school success. They posit that the challenge for educational leaders today is to remain focused on being a leader, rather than placing a heavy emphasis on managing schools. Literature linking the role of the school leader to student achievement and school effectiveness was comprehensively expounded upon, in Chapters 1 and 2.

Therefore, the specific focus was placed on providing aligned support that would help the principal participants with sustained opportunities to increase their skills as instructional leaders. It was felt that there was a strong correlation between the principals' effectiveness as a leader, and their ability to facilitate successful PLCs at their respective school sites. As part of the planning process, decisions were made to embed research-based practices in our Administrators' PLC that would emulate the necessary conditions reflected in a high-functioning Professional Learning Community.

CREATING A CULTURE OF INTERDEPENDENCE

Upon embarking on our early efforts in the Administrators' PLC, it was imperative that the participants, who comprised the principals, the central office superintendents, and the university facilitator, would work to establish interdependent relationships where continuous learning opportunities were provided and embraced. Matthews, Williams and Stewart (2007 in Matthews and Crow, 2010) describe the quality of interdependence as a focus on learning through shared classroom practices with their teachers that serve to foster and create a community of learners. It was our unwavering belief, that creating the condition of interdependence in our Administrators' PLC would help the principal participants understand this invaluable condition, which they in turn could emulate with their teachers in their PLCs at their respective school-sites.

CULTIVATING A COLLECTIVE MISSION AND SHARED SENSE OF PURPOSE

Another condition that was fostered pertained to the cultivation of a collective mission and shared sense of purpose, where evidence of shared-leadership practices were valued and implemented. While our mission was not solidified during our first year as an Administrators' PLC, the intention to cultivate and solidify our mission, vision, and shared sense of collective purpose was prevalent in our early work. We now have a PLC definition that reflects the voices of the principal participants and the teachers throughout the district. However, this was a formidable task which needed to remain at the forefront of our work. Attaining and embedding a collective sense of ownership in a shifting school culture where isolated and unaligned practices were prominent characteristics, required a focused, multi-year effort to solidify.

IMPLEMENTING RESEARCH-BASED PRACTICES

In view of the fact that it was of essence to ground our work in research-based practices, as it aligned to national and state principal competencies, the participants

CHAPTER 4

in the Administrators' PLC were introduced to the Southern Regional Educational Board (SREB) 13 Critical Success Factors. This work completed by SREB (2008) was indicative of some of the most current research on what principals needed to know and be able to do. It was also important to attain a focus based on a collective needs assessment from our participants. Since instructional leadership was perceived as one of the critical tenets for reaching the collective outcome of supporting teachers' growth that correlated to student achievement gains, three critical success factors were selected, which aligned to three of the state and national competencies. The SREB 13 critical factors and the process of embedding them into our work has been described in depth in Chapter 3.

DEVELOPING A FOCUS

While the participants in the Administrators' PLC felt that all of the 13 Critical Success Factors (CSF) was central to their role as successful school leaders, establishing a focus and making an initial needs assessment which would be revised as our work progressed was of essence. It was collectively determined that a priority of what we would work on would be established. The CSF that was selected closely aligned to the state and national competencies. The selection of these factors was an important first step for embedding and aligning our practices that would help us realize our outcome of building upon the participants' instructional capacity.

The Administrators' PLC was not formally in place until the latter part of the second year of the partnership. However, the work of the university-district partnership that led to this development, served to build a foundation for helping the participants solidify the connection between their role as instructional leaders and their ability to provide developmentally aligned assistance to their teachers for the overarching goal of increased student achievement levels.

BOOK STUDIES

As addressed in-depth in Chapter 3, the practice of embedding book studies in our Administrators' PLCs, was integral to building leadership capacity. The learning provided consistent opportunities for integrating theory and practice. As the participants became increasingly invested in their continuous learning process and gleaned value in the Administrators' PLC, greater decision-making on book selections and activities were evidenced.

BUILDING ON EXISTING STRUCTURES

During the time the district put in place PLCs and created a common PLC meeting time at the respective sites, principals were charged with conducting classroom walk-throughs on a regular basis. In an effort to help maximize the structures put in place and to help principals meet the varied developmental needs of teachers, a professional development tool was purchased for district-wide implementation. The segments centered on observing and discussing best practices which were modeled in video segments, and were viewed and discussed in our early sessions. One of the established goals for the first year of the Administrators' PLC was to conduct classroom walkthroughs as a group. As collective learners, we engaged in the first steps of what is still an ongoing process in our Administrators' PLC. Working to determine and implement the appropriate supervisory behaviors on a behavioral continuum (Glickman et al. 2010) as they connect to conducting effective instructional conversations that could change teachers' practice, is a fundamental component to our continued work.

CONCLUSION

This chapter formally introduced the principal participants. The voices of the principals were heard as they reflected on their principal preparation programs as well as their experiences with professional development once they became seated principals. The learning gleaned from the principal participants, served to inform our early work in the Administrators' PLC. The findings from the principals' perspectives were instrumental in guiding our continuous improvement efforts in response to the changing needs of the principals. The framework of the Administrators' PLC was designed to have fluidity within the structure, as it was important to be able to respond to the changing educational landscape centered on external forces that influenced the work of the Administrators' PLC.

Analyses of the emergent themes were provided, which had significant implications for guiding the early and continual efforts of the Administrators' PLC. Finally, within the context of the specific topics, the author shared the process of how our collective learning as a group guided our practice and continuous development in the Administrators' PLC.

Chapter 5 is centered on the question of understanding in what ways principals constructed their experiences and made meaning from their individual and collective knowledge, after engaging in a professional learning community model over a sustained period of time.

CHAPTER 5

CHANGED PRINCIPAL PERCEPTIONS

Chapter 4 formally introduced the principals and the contextual setting of the school district. The focus of Chapter 4 was to highlight the voices of the principals pertaining to their perceptions of their principal preparation programs. The learning gleaned from the emergent themes served to guide our early and progressive work in the Administrators' PLC which has commenced its fourth year as a PLC, and the fifth year as a university-district partnership.

Central to further exploring the question intended on understanding the specific ways that principals constructed their experiences and made meaning from the individual and collective knowledge acquired from job-embedded learning with their peers, was the learning gleaned from the participants' changed perceptions about being a principal. There was a collective interest in understanding if and to what extent the Administrators' PLC had made a difference in changing the participants' perceptions about what it meant to be a principal in a post NCLB era. We were similarly attentive to the tenets and dynamics that may have served to facilitate changed perceptions that affected impact. The analyses of the focal question in this chapter served to provide indicators associated between changing principals' practice that could positively affect the change of teachers' behaviors in the classroom.

This chapter was organized around two overarching inquires which unveiled several underlying themes. The partnership was intent on learning about the principals' initial thoughts and perceptions when they first participated in the Administrators' PLC. The second inquiry was centered on their individual and collective changed perceptions after participating in the Administrators' PLC. We felt that understanding the dynamics and processes embedded in these two topics was critical to understanding the effect changed perceptions may have on changing principal practice. The findings and discussion centered on the bearing of changed principal practice is addressed in depth in Chapter 6. The voices represented in this chapter incorporated individual interviews, foci groups, as well as the participants' viewpoints interspersed with conversations held in the Administrators' PLC. A discussion incorporating the author's perspectives on this process is embedded throughout the chapter.

INITIAL THOUGHTS ABOUT THE VALUE OF THE ADMINISTRATORS' PLC

When the participants were asked about their initial thoughts pertaining to their perceived value of sustained professional development for principals provided through the platform of the Administrators' PLC, two reoccurring themes became present. Most of the principal participants raised issues of relevance and uncertainty.

CHAPTER 5

Principal Savannah expressed her uncertainty through a metaphor that suggested a pattern of unsustainable professional development from her experience:

> It was another flavor of the month. One and done. It's gonna be here for a couple of weeks, or months, or whatever. And then it's gonna be done and we'll have something new next year, or next semester.

Principal Leticia expressed her trepidation about the relevance of the Administrators' PLC in this way:

> I accepted the position mid-year and my initial feeling was, "I don't have time for this." I was really worried because I was trying really hard to figure out what I needed to do at the school, and I did not see the value of this. Reflecting back, I now realize the importance of what I'm doing with staff development at my school is connected to the direction that the district is taking. Now I view this as a powerful way to move all of us in the right direction.

Principals Elisa and Natalia shared similar perceptions. Principal Elisa stated:

> I really didn't know what to expect. I didn't know what the group was going to be like, or what I was going to get out of this. At first, I resigned myself to saying, "here I am," wondering what I was going to become involved with.

Principal Natalia echoed Principal Elisa' initial reservations:

> That is essentially how I started. I came in, I sat and I listened, and honestly, I was kind of lost. I then went back to the office and found some of the facilitator's notes and materials. I started reading, and figured out that it was probably going to be something pretty useful that I could learn a lot from.

Principal Edward shared his ambivalence and frustration in the following way:

> I felt like I was kind of drowning. I did not understand the purpose of what we were trying to do. I kept struggling to get my head wrapped around this thing. Yet on the other hand, I appreciated the professional development because at least it was an attempt to provide me with direction. But I still felt frustration as I did not know where we were going and what we were really trying to achieve.

Principal Isidro expressed his initial assessment as another piece he needed to add to his already full plate.

> When we first began as a group, the Administrators' PLC was a brand new concept that was introduced to me. I have been a principal for eight years, and shared thoughts that were similar to my colleagues; "something new to add." But it turned out that it was something new that I needed to learn. Now I think that it is an excellent tool to helping a principal in becoming an instructional leader.

Principal Tiffany joined the Administrators' PLC after its conception. She was a retired principal who accepted the position of a middle school principal.

I joined the group after it had been in place for a while. Therefore I felt like I was swimming upstream when I first sat in the sessions. I was handed the books to read, and was expected to participate in the group sessions. I began to see this as an adventure. Then it became easy for me to want to catch up with other principals in this group. I eventually saw this as useful, and for me, usefulness is very important.

Reflecting on her practice post retirement, Principal Tiffany expressed:

After being retired, I can now see where the PLCs and the professional development provided for principals are certainly advantageous for running a school that can meet the needs and demands of the 21st century.

Principal Kurtis reflected on the topic of usefulness of the Administrators' PLC from a different perspective.

As a previous teacher who was in the classroom and participated as a member of a PLC, I have a different perspective. When I became an administrator and became involved in this process, I found it to be very useful. I felt that if we are to develop our direction, and develop our protocol as far as what we need to work on and accomplish, we need to work together within this PLC group.

Principal Kurtis discussed the developmental and ongoing nature of the Administrators' PLC.

We're still working through this process. We are all still developing—in the developmental process. And we are being able to work together and combine all of our resources here within the schools. As administrators, we are finding common ground, which I feel is necessary to be able to develop an effective PLC.

INSIGHTS ON PRINCIPALS' CHANGED PERCEPTIONS

Themes centered on changing perceptions of how the principals perceived the usefulness and relevance of their participation became increasingly observable after two years of the principals' participation in the Administrators' PLC. Prominent themes which became apparent from the principal participants were centered on moving away from isolation; embracing the growth process in shared practice; and cultivation of a shared vision as a group, which may have facilitated the practice of centralized instructional practices within the district. Another theme that became apparent pertained to the principals' changed perception of central office. Central office had made a sustained commitment to professional development through PLCs for the teachers and principals, which was acknowledged by some of the principal participants.

ISOLATION

Principal Natalia reflected on the usefulness of the Administrators' PLC as it pertained to the issue of isolation and isolated practices.

CHAPTER 5

> For me, I think this group has been important because I do not feel isolated. Before, I felt like I was practicing in isolation. Because you are at your own school, and you have all these issues that arise, and issues that you do not really talk to your teachers about. So it was nice to have a sounding board, being able to talk and share experiences with people who were facing similar issues. We were eventually able to problem-solve around those issues together.

In one of the Administrators' PLC sessions during this time period, Principal Natalia reflected on the complexity of changing a school culture which practiced isolation to a collaborative school culture without the leadership of the principal. She expressed her observation:

> I find it very hard to change the culture of isolation to collaboration with very little support or interaction from the principal. Being a facilitator for my two PLCs can be a full-time job. I am finding that you have to be prepared. The responsibility of the planning and facilitation has to eventually be shared with the group leaders within your school.

The former superintendent who also participated regularly in our Administrators' PLCs, added to Principal Natalia's reflection:

> There is a learning curve that occurs for this level of facilitation to be shared with teachers and for this process to happen.

Principal Elisa addressed the process of transitioning from isolated practices to the gradual cultivation of shared practice, which over time, led to the attainment of purposeful focus.

> In the past, the focus was on separate schools, like we were separate entities. We practiced in isolation and made many decisions in isolation. Now, we are not only looking within each school, we are examining issues from a district-wide lens. We are now asking questions like, "How can we implement more consistent practices across the district, with our teachers, with our students, and with our administrators?" We are slowly coming together to look at the whole picture, instead of just looking at an issue from the perspective of our school, as a separate entity.

SHARED PRACTICE

Principal Edward associated shared practice with his professional growth as a principal. His changed perception about the purpose and value of the Administrators' PLC served to substantiate the usefulness of shared practice. When Principal Edward commenced his participation in this group, he was unclear as to its purpose, and was not sure if it was a counseling session or a gripe session.

> I initially kept asking myself, "What is this?" "Is this group a gripe session?" "Is this group a counseling session?" I spent some time continuously asking

myself "What is the purpose of this group?" I also remember saying to myself, "I'm gonna do my own thing." Now, I can see how I have grown, because I see this group as working together to do what we need to do for our kids.

In his reflection, Principal Edward compared how he initially perceived the group's usefulness to reflect his new understanding of the group's purpose after two years of participation, reflective of his growth and changed perception. Principal Edward makes a viable connection between his charge as a principal and the need to impact student achievement. He now perceives the function of this group as a vehicle for impacting student success, and takes ownership in the process.

Now I can see how we have fine-tuned this process. This isn't necessarily as much for our teachers, but rather, the question becomes, "What are we doing as principals to help our teachers make sure that our students are successful and can attain the type of success that we envision for them?"

GROWTH PROCESS IN SHARED PRACTICE

After two years of sustained work as an Administrators' PLC, which marked the third year of the partnership, most of the principal participants began to make correlations between their individual and collective growth. This growth was attributed to, in part, participation in job-embedded shared practice. Shared practice over a sustained period of time facilitated the cultivation of a shared sense of purpose that led to refining the district mission and vision, in addition to centralizing and aligning district-wide practices. During the third year of the partnership, central office increasingly integrated the collective voices of the participants in much of the decision-making process. Evidence of these changed practices served to facilitate and solidify the shared vision and collective sense of shared purpose, which DuFour, DuFour, Eaker, and Many (2006) refer to as common ground.

OUTCOMES OF SHARED PRACTICE

The topic of shared-practice and the implications of sharing practice were central to the focus of another Administrators PLC session during the second year of implementation. As Principal Isidro reflected on the progress that this group has made throughout this journey, the Associate Superintendent asked a question pertaining to our collective mission. His question served to challenge our assumptions which pertained to disconnected practices.

What is our mission? Our practices do not currently fit with our current mission. Perhaps the next step would be to continue the PLC as a whole group and then work on revisiting the mission which would lead to cultivating a shared vision.

CHAPTER 5

CULTIVATION OF A SHARED VISION

The individual and collective internalization between the principals' perceptions of the usefulness of the Administrators' PLC brought to light the importance of shared practice. The sustainability of shared practice among the principal participants led to the eventual cultivation of a shared vision and common ground, facilitating an increase in aligned practices throughout the district and respective school sites. The principals referred to this alignment as centralized instructional practices within the district.

Principal Tiffany discussed the usefulness of the Administrators' PLC as it pertained to alignment and the establishment of common expectations that are increasingly reflected in the individual school sites.

> The usefulness of the Administrators' PLC as I see it is that principals are working on the same page now. Instead of the fragmentation that existed between principals' practice and each school being different, there is evidence of cohesiveness amongst the principals. We have been working together on our own professional development within the Administrators' PLC. So we're basically all developing the same set of expectations that are implemented when we return to our schools.

Principal Isidro expressed that we are now beyond the "storming and norming" phases that DuFour, DuFour, and Eaker (2008) reference in the stages involved in building a Professional Learning Community.

> Well, we have moved beyond the storming and norming stages. I think now we're getting to be very goal oriented. And we work together in teams. It took us a couple of years to realize what we were looking for, to determine what our goals as a group were. As a result, we are now taking this to our teachers in various campuses district-wide. This process continues to evolve. It's changing and evolving. Even our PLCs at our schools are changing and evolving. Our PLCs at my school have evolved beyond the "storming and norming" stages. Our teachers are finding that PLCs have a place in our school.

Principal Elisa expressed her perceptions between increased alignment and a cultivated shared vision this way:

> I think our process of participating in the Administrators' PLC for over two years has led to increased focus and more consistent practices. In the past, each school site was doing their own thing. Now, we have moved from only looking at the issues and goals of our own schools, and we are examining the issues from a district-wide lens. We are now asking, "What can we do to be more consistent across the district for our students and our teachers, and also with our administrators?" From my lens, this is what has really changed. "We are increasingly coming together and really looking at our practice, our schools and issues holistically, rather as separate entities."

Principal Savannah echoed sentiments similar to those of Principal Elisa. She made the correlation between increased cohesiveness and a common vision. The common vision, which has taken time to develop and internalize, is the collective focus on student learning.

> I concur that we have a common vision. At least now, we are no longer a disjointed group. The focus has become on the learning of students. "Now, one can see the clear picture, what we're doing, and why we are participating in ongoing professional development." Now when we go back and share this process and the purpose of this process with our teachers and staff, "We now have an understanding of what is happening. And we support that."

CENTRALIZED INSTRUCTIONAL PRACTICES

The theme of centralized instructional practices of the district surfaced in context to the discussion of shared practice which had an effect on cohesiveness, alignment, and a focus on student learning. Principal Kurtis expounded on his thoughts of what it meant to have centralized instruction within the district.

> The process of sustaining and improving the Administrator PLC process has led to the centralization of instruction within the district. While we recognize that each school has their own individual needs and individual goals, we are able to increasingly establish strong centralized goals, where there is commonality between each of the schools within the district.

Principal Kurtis continued his elaboration on the implementation of this process, which was a noted shift for district practice.

> When we meet administratively as an Administrators' PLC, we are able to look at each other and work off of each other. We are able to come to the table and discuss the same topics, even though we recognize that everyone is at a different level, or has differentiated needs. As a result, we are able to address some of the commonalities across the schools, develop more consistent strategies, and be able to help and support one another from this respect.

Principal Kurtis made an observation of the effect that centralized practices have had on how professional development decisions have changed district-wide.

> I strongly believe that the work together as an Administrators' PLC has helped with how we decide on district-wide professional development. We can actually see a really strong centralized goal that we share, which impacts the decisions that are made. There is commonality in the trainings and in-services for our teachers, regardless of the school. As a district, we are working on the same goals.

CHAPTER 5

The process of centralized instructional practices also entailed the alignment of the standards and the prioritization of power standards which are assessed by the state. This alignment has specific significance, as the timeline for the nationwide initiative of the Common Core State Standards has been implemented since the commencement of the Administrators' PLC. In addition to the implementation of the Common Core, the accountability system that measures the performance of schools and districts, have changed.

The state of New Mexico was one of the few states that applied for and was granted a waiver for NCLB accountability. The state has since developed its own accountability system, which comprises an "A to F" grading system. Prior to the grading system, school progress in New Mexico was based on NCLB Adequately Yearly Progress (AYP). This change has had an impact on trying to understand the formulas that the state utilizes for measuring school growth. It is the perspective of the university-district partnership that if the mechanism of the Administrators' PLC had not been in place, the systemic transition involving the Common Core Standards and the change in how each school's performance is now measured, would not have been as efficacious or timely.

Principal Natalia commented on the ability of the principals and district to adapt to external change forces that have included the change in how schools are measured, as well as the recent adoption of the Common Core Standards.

> Well, I think that the continuous professional development we are receiving is a natural response to the state and federal changes that are occurring. I believe the district has taken a really positive step. Instead of waiting until something is done that we do not have a clue about what's coming down the pike, we are trying to be proactive. We are working together to build on our foundation to help ensure that we'll be on board. And you know, it all comes back to the student. Taking a look at some of the future changes are and being ready for them is really important.

CONCLUSION

The focus of this chapter was centered on understanding how the principals perceived the relevance and applicability of the Administrators' PLC. The author commenced this chapter with highlighting the initial principal perceptions and understanding of the purpose and significance of engaging in sustained professional development as a district-wide effort. The findings centered on the principals' individual and collective changed perceptions after participating in the Administrators' PLC for two years was shared.

The author placed a focus on deeply understanding if and to what extent the sustained job-embedded professional development provided through the Administrators' PLC had made a difference in changing principals' perceptions, centered on what it meant to be a principal in an era marked by continuous accountability initiatives.

Reoccurring themes and successive themes which became apparent underscored the moving away from isolation; embracing the growth process in shared practice; the increasingly held value and importance of what it means to be an instructional leader; and the increased ability to make connections between the principal's role and student achievement.

The importance of reflecting on individual and collective practice and the gradual cultivation of a common purpose as principals changed their perceptions over time, were outcomes that were realized from the partnership's sustained efforts. An integral analysis induced from the emergent themes, which has implications for informing practice and research in the field, is that most of the participants in this project felt that it took two years of sustained work prior to the realization of the aforementioned outcomes.

Chapter 5 concluded with a discussion highlighting centralized instructional practices within the district, evidenced by the districts' increased capacity to proactively respond to and implement externally mandated state and federal initiatives. Chapter 6 paid specific attention to the themes providing indication of principals' changed priorities, which had a bearing on the changing direction of the district. Chapter 6 also shared specific examples of principals' participation in the Administrators' PLC, which has served to facilitate a change in the thinking of what it now means to be a principal. Several themes emerged which provided indicators reflecting changed principal participants' priorities. A discussion and analyses of the themes has been embedded into this chapter.

CHAPTER 6

IMPACT ON PRACTICE

Central to the theme in Chapter 5, was to convey the ideas and beliefs of principals' initial thoughts pertaining to the relevance of their participation in professional development delivered through the formation of the Administrators' PLC. Findings of principals changed perceptions were included in the chapter. The chapter was concluded with a discussion which highlighted the implications that changed principal perceptions had for both the principal participants and the central office.

Chapter 6 paid special attention to understanding the connection between changed principal perceptions, principal behaviors, and priorities. The bearing these changes had on their practice as a principal were revealed through the participants' voices. Several themes emerged that provided indication of how principal participants' thinking of what it now means to be a principal has changed.

PRINCIPAL OWNERSHIP FOR BUILDING TEACHER CAPACITY

An emergent theme centered on learning in what ways that participating in the Administrators' PLC had facilitated a change in practice, was centered on the participants' increased level of ownership to build teacher capacity. The principal participants addressed specific ways that building teacher capacity was operationalized into practice.

Principal Elisa reflected on how the learning in the Administrators' PLC served to change her practice which involved moving away from the praxis of directing teachers to providing teachers with differentiated levels of guidance and support.

> You know, I used to always be telling teachers what to do. And as a principal who has engaged in the process of the PLC, I now think a little differently. I think that my role should be to provide specific support and guidance. It's kind of like when you're teaching kids, you feel you have to give them the answer. And I feel like in my role as a principal, I've learned to slowly step back, and provide opportunities for teachers to figure out a specific problem for themselves. In many cases, I feel that this approach is more powerful than just telling them what to do, or directing them.

CHANGE IN PRINCIPAL BEHAVIORS AND PRIORITIES

Throughout our sustained work as a group, we observed that principals' behaviors and priorities changed as they became more comfortable with their role as instructional

CHAPTER 6

leader. The skills associated with the role of instructional leader required an emphasis on collaboration, visibility, listening skills, communication, shared practice, and an increased need to develop interdependent relationships with their teachers. These observations were noted over a sustained period of time, as the university-district partnership had multiple opportunities to observe principals' interactions with their teachers.

Additional indicators that provided evidence of principals' changed behaviors that facilitated a change in practice, were provided through the interactions in the Administrators' PLC. In addition, conversations and activities that occurred during the individualized coaching sessions between each principal and the facilitator, provided opportunities for continuous annotation of changed behaviors that were associated with changed practice. The multifaceted opportunities to collect data on principals changed behaviors provided indication that principals demonstrated an increased ability to provide teachers with opportunities to take risks, make self-assessments, and have teachers take increased ownership in their practice.

Principal Elisa continued her reflection:

> While we need to provide continuous guidance for our teachers, I need my teachers to feel confident in their own thinking, be able to look at their own data, and have the "light-bulb turn on," where they say, "I can see why I am getting these results and how using the data can help me make certain changes." I want this to increasingly come from our teachers.

Principal Kurtis reflected on his changed practice as it connected with building teacher capacity in the following way:

> I think that my ability to look at things particularly in teaching and learning in a more critical manner, to be able to go in with some real objective criteria for what makes good instruction, for what makes a good classroom environment, and for what makes effective learning for students, has improved. As an administrator, paying attention to these factors when I go into the classroom has become much easier and much clearer. Now when I observe a teacher, I have a much better idea of what it is I am looking for, and feel more confident in helping the teacher to improve her practice.

A crucial theme that was brought to the forefront was the recognition that teaching practice needs to look differently in an effort to more closely meet the diverse needs of students in the 21st century.

Principal Tiffany commented:

> I do not feel that we are ready to teach 21st century kids. We're gonna have to teach to them subjects and provide them with skill-sets for future positions that do not yet exist. I think that the PLC process is going to help keep us on track as we make the necessary changes for meeting the needs of students in the 21st century. I do not have all of the answers, because the technology

that our students will be exposed to in ten years could be mind-blowing. However, I know that both the Administrators' PLC and the Teachers' PLC are platforms that could help keep us focused on student-centered needs and practices. Knowing that these kids are 21st century kids, we need to be on top of everything. I'm excited about this kind of stuff."

SUPPORTING STUDENT-CENTERED PRACTICES THROUGH THE FACILITATION OF PLCS

Another theme that supported the perception of engaging in student-centered practices was the increased connection between the principal's role and their charge to increase the efficacy of the PLCs at their respective school-sites.

Principal Natalia indicated:

Well, a big focus for me is our team PLC meetings at my school. I am really feeling that this is my priority at our school right now. Admittedly, not everyone has totally gotten on board. Some are being compliant; they are going to their team meetings and things like that. But we are in the process of setting norms for each team, and goals. And really, as I'm learning, I'm helping to facilitate a lot better. I feel that we have a better direction.

Principal Natalia continued:

And so it just takes a lot of time and preparation, until the teachers become more independent. I see this as my role to facilitate those meetings and to make sure that the work is happening. It is important that the work is of quality. I do not want the teachers to say "Oh, yeah, we're meeting just because we have to." Rather, we are meeting because this is good for our school, this is what is good for our students, and this is what is good for us. As educators, it is gonna help us to improve.

PRINCIPALS TAKING OWNERSHIP OF STUDENT SUCCESS

Principal Natalia's reflection is indication that she assumes responsibility for her students' success, as a result of the effective facilitation of the Teachers' PLCs at her school. She has a deeper appreciation for the change process, and the learning curve involved for teachers. Unequivocally, she perceives her role as pivotal to facilitating effective PLCs that can help teachers improve and change behaviors that correlate to meeting students' needs.

Principal Tiffany's reflection resonated closely with that of Principal Natalia.

I continuously ask myself if what we are doing is really preparing our students for the real world. Are we preparing students to have specific goals when they graduate? If they do not have a goal, then I feel that I have not done my job. While a student can change his goal, he is at least working towards something.

CHAPTER 6

> If he does not have a sense of direction or purpose, he is more likely to go on the streets, and he will struggle more. But if I can provide him, we as a team can provide him with the conditions for attaining a goal, and support him while he is in high school; he is more likely to succeed.

Additional themes that provided indication of changed principals' perceptions as it connected to changed practices and priorities, included themes of embracing continuous improvement; accountability; value of shared practice; increased receptivity of input from parents and community stakeholders; the value of research to guide continuous improvement; and the shift from manager to instructional leader. The analyses of these themes, suggested that the principals had made connections between the aforementioned tenets which emerged from the themes as necessary for serving as a principal defined by the literature of what today's principal needs to know and be able to do.

ENGAGING THE VOICES OF PARENTS AND THE COMMUNITY

Principal Tiffany continued her reflection by making the connection between her role as principal and the need to value input from parents and the community for the sake of the student.

> And it's sad, but if you get parents involved, your school will succeed. If this is not happening in my school, I feel that it is up to me. "I ask myself, why should I not have parental, community, and business input?" I need to be able to ask these stakeholders, "what do you want?" While I do not like to put it into these terms, the school turns out a product in the end; it is the student. Therefore, we must look at this from that perspective.

SHARED PRACTICE AND CONTINUOUS IMPROVEMENT

Principal Alecia made the connection between shared practices that are now taking place in the Administrators' PLC as well as in Teachers' PLCs. In her reflection, she addressed the ways that shared practice facilitated individual and collective improvement effort.

> In our Administrators' PLCs, there is more sharing, more documentation of what we share, as we follow an agenda that guides our discussions. I think the level of sharing is more sincere and focused. We address issues we are dealing with in our schools, and what the principals need in terms of support, so we can address these issues.

Principal Alecia addressed the development of this shared process as it correlated to facilitating opportunities for continued growth.

> I think when we talk about issues within our schools, the feelings of inadequacy and embarrassment have been diminished. Before, we worked in isolation and

were concerned about our colleagues knowing what we were going through with teachers, parents, or whatever the issue was. I now feel that there is a comfort level that we did not have before, and we now see each other more as a support team. I think the more we go through this process, the more we feel we can lean on each other and learn from each other, as we are not working in isolation.

Principal Alecia spoke to the issue of competiveness that was present prior to the implementation of the Administrators' PLC.

> The biggest change that I have noticed since we began this process is that competitiveness existed between the schools. There are four elementary schools in our district, and it was like, "ok, my elementary school is going to outshine the other three elementary schools." The individual principals were focused on their test scores outshining the other principals' test scores.

SHARED PRACTICE TO ALIGN EFFORTS THROUGHOUT THE pK-12 DISTRICT PIPELINE

Principal Alecia brought to light that a significant change in behavior and practice between the principals was the noted shift in my school, engaging in a team effort that supported the improvement of all schools.

> Probably the biggest change that both PLC structures brought about was that this is "not just about my school." It is about our team and all of our schools within the district.

The collective shift in thinking had a bearing on aligning practices that would consider the educational pipeline from elementary school through high school. Principal Alecia continued:

> We have come to the realization that our middle school is a feeder school for the four elementary schools. Therefore, it is no longer about our kids while they are with us in the elementary schools. The focus is now on needing to work hard to make sure that when these students transition to middle school, they can perform just as well in the middle school, as they did when these kids were here, at the elementary school.

Principal Alecia concluded her thoughts on the effects of working together to share practice that facilitated the ability to look at the system at large, that incorporates the separate, yet interdependent school within the district:

> I believe this process has led to a sense of camaraderie. There is an increased feeling of trust as we have moved away from working in isolation, and are sharing practices that help our students.

Principal Leticia shared her insights regarding shared practice, which she associated with the collaborative process.

CHAPTER 6

> Well you know, I have always believed in collaboration. I value collaboration with my colleagues as well. As a principal prior to coming here, I worked hard at trying to get teacher input. I always felt like a school should be run as a team. Every job that I had, I tried hard to run my department as a team.

Principal Leticia continued the conversation by connecting how the Administrators' PLC helped her to become more efficacious with a core belief she had prior to engaging in the job-embedded learning as a team.

> So, being in a PLC, and learning more about it, I think I do this better. I feel more confident with the process of collaboration at my school. Our PLC has provided me with a lot of good ideas that I am able to bring back and share with my teachers here at my school.

While Principal Leticia values the process of shared-practice that occurs in a collaborative setting, she also spoke to the resistance that is felt by some of her teachers:

> I still have some teachers that are a little bit resistant to collaboration. However, I am working on this with these teachers.

EMBRACING CONTINUOUS IMPROVEMENT TO IMPACT STUDENT ACHIEVEMENT

Principal Natalia spoke to the connection between embracing the continuous improvement process and student achievement.

> We're meeting in both PLCs because this is what is good for our school. This is what is good for our students. This is what is good for us. I believe this process will help all of us as educators to improve. And that's the goal; the goal is to continue for continuous improvement.

In Principal Natalia's reflection, she realized the need for her own continuous improvement process in an effort to help teachers grow and improve their practice that can make a difference in student achievement.

> I think I have realized that I have to continue to learn. I have to continue to learn, and I want to continue to learn. It is important for me to become better at what I am doing. And I want to help teachers become better at what they are doing as well. Our improvement helps to impact student achievement.

Principal Natalia continued her reflection centered on the need for her continuous growth and the need for teachers to embrace the continuous learning process:

> I'm learning, but I'm not where I want to be. And I'm hoping that my teachers feel that way as well. Honestly, I think some of the teachers feel like they know it all and they are great at what they do. Therefore, they do not need to continue to learn. And that is just not the case. Unfortunately, there are too many times when we are teaching and students are not learning. And that's where the gap happens.

IMPACT ON PRACTICE

Principal Natalia concluded her reflection:

> And that's where we need to focus on and make sure that we do not have gaps in our teaching and in our learning. If we do have gaps, then we must ask ourselves, "what are we going to do about it?"

CONNECTING RESEARCH TO CONTINUOUS IMPROVEMENT

As principals made the connection between the process of acquiring new skill sets that influenced how they practiced, remaining current on research and best practices became a priority.

Principal Natalia expressed her realization in the following way:

> Well, I want to say that I've realized how important research that others do that inform our practice. I understand the importance of staying abreast with the literature by reading, and looking at what is being done. I am also interested in practices that work. Therefore, I want to know what other schools are doing; other PLCs that have been successful. I think that this is something of importance: all of those discussions that we have about the research that's out there. Also, attending the PLC Conference in Las Vegas was very beneficial. Practices like that, are continually helping me to become the leader that I want to be.

CONNECTIONS BETWEEN ACCOUNTABILITY AND CHANGED PRACTICE

Throughout our collective experiences in working with the principals, we have observed that principals increasingly appreciate the relevance of using data to inform practice. The following assertion made by Principal Tiffany, speaks to how she has integrated the use of data to inform her practice. As importantly, she perceived the relevance and importance of placing a focus on being held accountable for showing student results, as it connected to impacting student achievement.

> In some ways, my role as principal has become more complicated. In other ways, the use of data, the need to progress monitor, has brought a level of concreteness into my job. For me, it is more concrete, it is more black and white. When I was a principal before retirement, we looked at the records, and we looked at the scores. However, you were not held accountable to what you needed to do next. For me, the piece that has changed my practice is that "I am now enthusiastic about showing results." With progress monitoring, I can show where the specific student successes are. And that is a new change for me. We did not have this before.

As Principal Tiffany continued her reflection, she made the following assertion pertaining to the role of accountability and the ways it is changing her practice as a principal.

CHAPTER 6

> My practice as a principal is changing because of the PLCs. I believe that if you are not held accountable, one can slack off as well. The PLCs from my perspective, can keep you from slacking off, if you are running them correctly, and if you attend them with the right frame of mind. The materials we are asked to read which help us to grow, do not always provide sufficient knowledge. However, it prompts me to go on the internet and research a specific topic further. The process of being held accountable to further my growth has given me insight into what the teachers collaboratively need to be doing and what they need to be held accountable for. The use of data helps me to assess where we are and where we need to go. This is a whole new realm in education. I think being held accountable in the long run is going to be what we need, in order to make students more successful.

THE PARADIGM-SHIFT FROM MANAGER TO INSTRUCTIONAL LEADER

An important outcome of the Administrators' PLC was to help provide the conditions that could assist the principals to understand the tenets required to perform effectively as an instructional leader. As indicated earlier in this book, this process has required a multi-year effort, as the shift embeds second-order change principles. The behaviors that provided indicators that the principals were exhibiting behaviors associated with an instructional leader, were evidenced with greater consistency during the second year of the Administrators' PLC.

Principal Kurtis spoke to the process which involved this transition:

> I think that the discussion has been going on in our state for several years now, pertaining to the role of the principal changing from serving as the building manager to that of instructional leader. One element that I see changing both in our district as well as statewide, to some extent, is that principals are becoming instructional leaders. I see this happening more in our district, primarily as a result of engaging in this process.

Principal Kurtis continued to address the tenets he perceived were associated with the role of instructional leader.

> The instructional leaders are providing regular assessment of what is occurring in the individual classrooms. They are working with teachers on developing effective instructional strategies. These are some of the components that really help to make the principal an instructional leader as opposed to just the building manager.

Principal Kurtis closed his reflection on this discussion with the following comment:

> I now see a lot more of this type of practice going on here in our district than I used to see here. I also observed that these practices occur more in our district than in other schools that I have observed, which are outside of our district.

IMPACT ON PRACTICE

Principal Isidro addresses the shift from serving primarily as a building manager to that of an instructional leader. He addressed how this shift has completely changed his practice.

> I think that you know, I started in administration before accepting this position as a secondary principal. In my mind, and from my perspective, serving as an instructional leader is a complete change in how I perceived the principal's role. Perhaps this is not a change in perception for the public, or for other administrators within school systems. For me, when I started out, I was the building manager. And even back then, the best principals did try to focus on instructional issues. When I was a beginning principal, I did try to focus on some of those instructional issues. But in those days, you were considered to be the building manager. Now, this has completely changed.

In Principal Natalia's reflection pertaining to her role as instructional leader, she commented on the function of the Administrators' PLC, as well as the PLCs at her respective site.

> First of all, the PLCs help me to focus on the priorities that my job of instructional leader, entails. Therefore, I've been able to find a balance between the management and instructional leadership part of it.

Principal Natalia attributed her ability to balance the role of instructional leadership and management, to the learning and support she receives from her colleagues as they share practice. She also expressed her opinion that the Administrators' PLCs served as a platform for her to share evidence with her colleagues pertaining to the work that is occurring in the PLCs at her respective sites.

> I have learned from other administrators. As I mentioned earlier, the learning in large part, is contributed to all of the sharing that happens in the Administrators' PLC. We share evidence of the work that is occurring, and the progress being made at our PLCs in our schools. Therefore, I am constantly thinking about, what I will share at our PLC.

CHANGING CONVERSATIONS WITH TEACHERS

An outcome of our sustained focus on increasing principals' efficacy as instructional leaders has facilitated a shift in the type of conversations that principals have with teachers.

Principal Isidro offered the following insight:

> Now look at our PLCs. We have discussed academic rigor, and the relevance of academic rigor for making a difference in student achievement. Personally, I had never heard about academic rigor. Now I ask, "do we have academic rigor at our school?" I believe we do. However, I do not think that our teachers realized we had academic rigor, or really knew anything about it. They certainly

CHAPTER 6

did not know how to make connections between academic rigor and student achievement. It was never brought up before our involvement in our own PLC.

Principal Natalia provided a specific example of her changed principal practice. She described specifically how her increased ability to improve her questioning skills with her teachers has changed the focus of her conversations.

> I think one of the things that this process has done, is to help me improve my questioning with teachers, and the type of conversations I have with teachers. My conversations are about student achievement, about practices within the classroom; pertain to strategies that they are using, the SAT process, and the RtI process. All of these factors now come into play in our PLCs as well. And I think that becoming more knowledgeable about these topics helps me be able to share these things with my teachers.

INTENTIONAL PRACTICE WITH A FOCUS ON OUTCOMES

A related theme to an observed shift in the type of conversations principals had with their teachers was centered on the priority to become intentional in their practice. A focus on results has been a reoccurring tenet, threaded in several of the emergent themes. This focus on results and outcomes is highlighted in the following reflections.

Principal Isidro provided his reflection regarding the topic of teacher efficacy, making the connection between this principle and student efficacy.

> Teachers did not realize the importance of teacher efficacy. I believe that if we have teacher efficacy, it can be transmitted to student efficacy. If we can delve more into this area, we will really succeed as a school.

Principal Isidro continued his reflection, posing several questions centered on the necessary tenets for attaining intended outcomes.

> I raised the question regarding our teaching framework. That was never discussed before. We brought this to light and talked about this.

He referenced the dialogue he had with his teachers, centered on the questions that prompted a discussion regarding the teacher's framework.

Teachers began to wonder, and raised the question, "What happened before?" Principal Isidro responded:

> You were doing things. But you did not realize what you were doing. With a school teaching framework in place, it provides us with the structure to help ensure that everything we do is aligned with our standards and benchmarks. We have to have guidance; the framework is our guidance.

As Principal Isidro continued his reflection, similarly to his colleagues, increased student achievement and student outcomes, were his focus.

> We have to be concerned with how we teach, as we have one goal in mind. This goal pertains to student outcomes. We need to ensure that we achieve increased student success.

Principal Isidro referenced the model of Wiggins and McTighe's Backward Design, which was introduced in Chapter 3. He referenced this model as it connected with the practice of using formative assessments for addressing student needs.

> The use of backward design helps us to establish our outcomes and goals, and work backwards. We are working with formative assessments to inform our practice, as it connects to the outcomes we have established.

As Principal Isidro reflected on the process of using the model to align practices, he addressed issues of efficacy with using formative assessments. He also indicated that he is working with his teachers to become more confident with using formative assessments, as well as intentional.

> Our teachers realize that we are using formative assessments. I believe that formative assessments should guide the way teachers teach. But I do not believe that all teachers are on board with this. I also question, "are we using formative assessments correctly?" "How intentional are we regarding the use of formative assessments?"

INTERPRETIVE ANALYSES FROM THE VOICES OF THE PRINCIPALS

My interpretative analyses of the assertions made through the perspectives of the principals was centered on the principle of acquiring efficacy. As principals obtained new skills sets and dispositions, and challenged old assumptions, they became increasingly confident and efficacious. Their perceived effectiveness facilitated a paradigm-shift in thinking and in practice, which varied between principals. I inferred that this process was a necessary prerequisite in order for the principals to internalize and embrace the value of shared practice and continuous learning.

As the principals progressed through the continuous development of the Administrators' PLC, I observed an increased sense of urgency to affect student achievement and address learning gaps. The outcome that purposefully informed their practice became centered on making a difference in student achievement. This was evidenced in Principal Natalia posing the question, "If there are gaps in learning and in teaching, what are we going to do about it?" An increasingly observed tenet threaded throughout these themes was connected to the principal's role, centered on making a difference in context to the teaching and learning at their respective sites.

As a facilitator and participant in this 5-year project, I discerned that the principals' collective change in thinking and in practice, aided the changing direction and decision making processes of the district. The principals' voices became more cohesive and focused on making decisions that were aligned with the district office and the changing needs that had an impact on the district as well as the school sites.

CHAPTER 6

While the principals were still concerned about decisions and practices that affected their sites, they became more intentional about engaging in a decision-making process with the district that spanned the scope of their individual schools. Their changed practice in this context reflected a global assessment.

The principals strived to align practices, policies and initiatives that considered the district, as well as the individual school sites. This observation was one powerful indicator that the principals were thinking and practicing in a systemic context. The collective decision making process increasingly became the cultural norm. As the principals and central office participants have worked together to cultivate a shared common purpose that impacts the pK-12 system within the district, the principle of interdependence within the system has been embedded.

CONCLUSION

This chapter focused on highlighting the critical links between the participants' changed perceptions about their role as principal, and the influence the changed behaviors have had on changing the practice of the principals. Several emergent themes were highlighted, discussed and analyzed. The chapter concluded with interpretive analyses based on the findings which emerged.

Chapter 7 explored the perceptions of the principal participants, as it concerned the sustained effort of the university-district partnership. In this chapter, the principals shared their insights concerning their involvement with the university, which strived to build leadership capacity through the development and implementation of the Administrators' PLC. The principals shared their individual and collective suggestions pertaining to topics of delivery, outcomes, impact, replication and sustainability. The findings from the emergent themes have implications for informing practice that involves universities, school districts and policymakers. These findings centered on providing job-embedded professional development that involves a university-district effort. These findings can promote the advancement of research in an area that warrants further inquiry.

CHAPTER 7

PRINCIPALS' PERCEPTIONS OF THE UNIVERSITY-DISTRICT PARTNERSHIP

Chapter 6 focused on highlighting the critical links between the participants' changed perceptions about their role as principal, and the influence the changed behaviors have had on changing the practice of the principals. Special consideration was given to understanding the connection between changed principal perceptions, principal behaviors, and priorities. Several themes emerged that provided an indication of how principal participants' thinking of what it now means to be a principal has changed. The bearing these changes had on their practice as a principal were revealed through the participants' voices. The chapter concluded with providing interpretive analyses on the findings which emerged from the themes.

Chapter 7 explored the perceptions of the principal participants, as it concerned the sustained effort of the university-district partnership. In this chapter, the principals shared their insights concerning their involvement with the university, which endeavored to build leadership capacity through the development and implementation of the Administrators' PLC. The principals shared their individual and collective insights pertaining to the outcomes of their individual and collective experiences.

The participants provided insights on the conditions necessary for sustaining the partnership, addressed barriers, and provided recommendations for facilitating continuous improvement efforts. The findings from the emergent themes have implications centered on issues of continuous improvement, replication, and sustainability. The inferences of these findings were expected to promote the advancement of research in an area that warrants further inquiry. Therefore, these findings reflecting the perceptions of the principal participants have implications for informing practice that involves universities, school districts, and policymakers.

SEGMENTS OF INQUIRY

This chapter was organized around three areas of inquiry. The intent was to provide a deeper understanding of the participants' perceptions centered on receiving job-embedded professional development provided through the sustained efforts of a university-district partnership. The three areas of inquiry were: receiving professional development from the partnership which involved a facilitator representing a higher education institution; perceived barriers; and recommendations for continuous improvement. Within the scope of this inquiry, several themes emerged, which have been analyzed and discussed in depth.

CHAPTER 7

INQUIRY CENTERED ON THE PARTNERSHIP WITH AN INSTITUTION OF HIGHER EDUCATION

Cultivated Conditions Necessary for Building a Team

Several themes surfaced which were relevant to understanding the connection between the learning of the participants and the involvement with a university facilitator. Principal Natalia addressed her ability to feel comfortable asking questions, and sharing perceptions:

> We have a lot of confidence that we can ask any question, we can share anything. There isn't anything that we cannot talk about, and never felt like we were asking a wrong question.

Condition of Comfort

Principal Natalia connected the importance of having the comfort level to communicate openly as it connected to developing a team and a shared sense of purpose.

> When you work as a team, you have one goal. No matter what the goal is, you set your goals. And, if you work as a team, I believe there is not much that you cannot accomplish. You are then on the same page.

Principal Natalia reflected on the importance of differences. Despite differences, you can still have a cultivated sense of purpose that is shared among the team members, "We're all different. Thank God we're all different."

Elaborating on the necessary condition of developing a level of comfort between the team members, Principal Natalia reflected on her need to feel comfortable with the facilitator.

> Feeling comfortable with the facilitator was important. I think that happened skillfully. The facilitator from the university came in with a plan. She had questions.

Condition of Placing Oneself in the Context of Learner

Principal Natalia, made reference to the ability of the facilitator to learn from the team, "I think she learned from us, but we learned from her."

Condition of Knowledge and Relevance

Principal Natalia referenced the condition of knowledge that the facilitator provided.

> She had the knowledge. She presented her knowledge in different ways. She had a plan. She had a plan. She brought us in step-by-step. But we were also challenged.

Principal Tiffany shared her insights centered on the tenets of knowledge and relevance, which she perceived to be necessary conditions.

> My intelligence needs to be challenged. I am not suggesting that I am that intelligent. However, I do not want to sit and waste my time. If I'm going to sit in sessions, I need to walk out of there saying, "Ah. Wow, I just learned something."

As Principal Tiffany continued with her reflection, she alluded to her assumptions of being challenged, as well as her thinking. For Principal Tiffany, these conditions were necessary if she was to find the learning within the context of the Administrators' PLC relevant.

> The facilitator, whom we have now, is always throwing things out there that challenge us. And so I appreciate that. Within the conversations that take place in our sessions, my intelligence and ideas are challenged with the concepts that are thrown at me. And then I can ask questions and work on that. I am not going to sit there and be "spoon-fed." I want and need to be challenged.

Condition of Serving in the Role of Principal

Principals Natalia, Tiffany, and Kurtis shared their perceptions pertaining to what they perceived as necessary prerequisites for an effective university-district partnership.

Principal Kurtis asserted his perception pertaining to the facilitator having served in the trenches as a building principal.

> I think the partnership works only because the partner from the university has been where we are today. It's not going to work with somebody who has been out of the loop. It is not going to work with somebody who hasn't been in the trenches.

Principal Natalia provided additional insights.

> We were really fortunate to have a facilitator who had experience as a principal. She had previous experience, and was skilled in leadership techniques. She brought these skills and techniques to us.

Condition of Building Relationships

Principal Kurtis embedded additional prerequisites he perceived as critical tenets.

> It is also not going to work with somebody who does not care. And this is what I like about what we have now. We have someone who cares. We have someone who listens. We have someone who works with us and tries to help us improve.

Principal Isidro's reflections on this condition resonated with those of Principal Kurtis.

> It was the way it was introduced to us. It was not shoved down our throats. It was presented to us. She communicated the ways that she could help, what she could provide, and how we can learn from each other as a team working on a common goal.

Principal Isidro continued:

> It involved sharing, getting to know who we are individually and as a group. She cares about who we are and what our needs are. If she presented herself in a manner that communicated, "I'm sitting over here and I have all of the knowledge, and you are all going to do what I say." This approach would have never worked.

Condition of Facilitator Associated With a University

The principal participants provided varied responses that corresponded with this condition.

Principal Isidro made this assertion: "I do not think that a facilitator not tied to a university can help us achieve where we are at."

Principal Savannah shared her insights as they pertained to the importance of the university to be involved with partnerships. She as well as other participants felt that the university has the capacity to bring in and share resources. It was also perceived that the university can benefit from the learning, as it can enhance their leadership preparation programs. The tenets of reciprocal learning, shared practice, and interdependence were woven through these conversations: "Well, I think that this is outstanding. This is particularly valuable if the institute of higher learning is utilizing their involvement to enhance their programs as well."

Principal Savannah underscored the benefits of the university's involvement centered on building leadership capacity with the districts. Their charge to design, deliver, and improve principal preparation programs, was at the core of her reflection.

> Universities are delivering administrator preparation programs. And I think for them to actually work in the public schools, and see what is going on firsthand, and to talk and meet with practicing administrators in the field, should enhance their program. I know that the university involvement has enhanced our programs.

Principal Elisa provided a slightly different perspective on this perceived condition.

> Well, he or she does not have to represent an institution from higher education. But at the same time, when you have higher education involved, it also makes us, practitioners in the public schools, feel like we are being 'challenged by higher education' institutions.

Principal Leticia offered the following insight:

> It is not to say that having a facilitator who does not represent a university cannot work. However, a facilitator not working in the capacity of the university may not have all of the knowledge and experience, and may not have access to research. However, she may still be of value to us.

Principal Leticia indicated her preference of having a facilitator associated with a university, as facilitators representing a university have access to other professors, graduate students, and ongoing research. This degree of involvement served to raise her confidence level.

> I feel confident to have the facilitator from the university, as she knows what's going on. She works with other professors. She works with graduate students, and their research. She works with students in general, and is very involved. Therefore, I feel that it is important to have her share her knowledge and experiences with us.

Condition of Central Office Leadership

In reflecting on the necessary conditions that served to facilitate the learning for the principal participants, Principal Natalia expressed the need for central office leadership, vision, and commitment.

> But we also had one leader in the administrative team, the associate superintendent. He shared the vision with the university. He participated in our Administrative PLC, and provided us with ideas.

Condition of Overcoming Differences

Principal Natalia spoke to the importance of working as a team in order to work through differences, "We didn't always agree. But we were able to work as a team for the purpose of fulfilling the outcomes of our established mission and vision within our district and schools."

Condition of Non-Negotiable Tenets

Principal Natalia conveyed that in light of variable dynamics, non-negotiable tenets must be present.

> There are a lot of variables. These variables include: personality, skill, knowledge, and teamwork. If you do not have an idea of what it is needed to develop a team, you're not going to have a team!

CHAPTER 7

Condition of Time

Principal Natalia noted the caveat of time. She made the connection between the necessary skills involved to develop and sustain an effective team, with the provision that necessary time and effort were dedicated for the development of the team.

> If you have the skills on how to develop a team, it will take about two to three years to develop a team. However, once you have achieved a solid team, you can really accomplish a lot of things that need to be done."

Principal Natalia's assertion pertaining to the length of time she perceived was required for developing a solid team connected by a shared purpose, served to support my analyses. In Chapter 3, the voices of principal participants centered on the activities and conversations in the Administrators' PLC provided additional indicators to support this assertion. Throughout my facilitation of the Administrators' PLC, I had indicated that the significant changes in principal behaviors that connected to changed practice were not consistently observed until the second year of the Administrators' PLC.

Data collected from the partnership's sustained participation with the principals, influenced our continuous assessment and decision making process. The decision to wait until the latter part of the second year to accompany the team of principals to the Professional Learning Communities Institute was centered on the premise expressed by Principal Natalia. The partnership believed that establishing the tenets of a cohesive team who took ownership of the underlying philosophical tenets that comprised a professional learning community, may increase the probability of attaining intended outcomes. It was important that the partnership would be able to collect evidence that the principals were able to integrate concepts learned at the Institute, and put them into practice at their respective sites. Another outcome was the expectation that the principals would be able to increase the level of their support provided to teachers, as it connected to increasing the level of impact of the PLCs at their respective sites.

Perceived Outcomes

A category which emerged pertained to what principals perceived as outcomes, reflective of the university-district partnership efforts. Several themes that corresponded to the category of perceived outcomes included: focus; powerful conversations; self-reflection; mentorship; and opportunities for reciprocal learning.

Focus

Principal Edward reflected on how he perceived the partnership facilitated an increased level of focus.

> I think we really have a good partnership with higher education. We have someone from the outside who participates in our PLCs. This brings us back

and makes us focus on things. This process also helps to bring our attention on issues from a different perspective, than what we were initially looking at.

Principal Edward continued his reflection on the topic of focus as he described the process:

> I think the process of being provided a different perspective is important. Sometimes we might be out in left field. Having someone who has a different set of experiences might throw something out there during our discussion. This helps to focus our thinking and to look at something a little differently.

Principal Edward's concluding thoughts on the topic of focus were centered on the questions which were presented, intended to clarify the direction of the participants.

> We needed to focus on what we as a district needed to do. Questions that we were continuously asked were, "Where do you need to go as a district?" "What are your student outcomes?" "Where do you think your teachers are, and where do you think they need to be?" "How might you get them there?"

Principal Edward perceived that the questioning helped to facilitate a focus which was shared by most participants in the PLC, "Having someone with knowledge to guide our focus has been an asset to us. Without this support, I think that we'd probably be still lost."

Powerful Conversations

As Principal Edward continued his reflection, he referenced his experience with the coaching he received, which supplemented his learning in the Administrators' PLC.

> Collaborating with the university facilitator has helped us to self-reflect on our practice. Having those professional discussions individually with the facilitator and with our colleagues, have been powerful. It has helped to improve our practice.

Mentorship

As Principals Natalia and Edward reflected on perceived outcomes centered on powerful conversations, focus, and mentoring, the tenet of facilitator knowledge was threaded into these themes.

Principal Natalia reflected on the outcome of mentorship as it aided her learning process, "Having a PLC mentor with so much knowledge, and willing to work with us, has been a huge plus for the district. It is hard to measure it."

Reciprocal Learning as a Team

The tenet of learning shared by stakeholders has been threaded throughout the themes that connect to the first segment of inquiry: receiving professional development from the partnership that involved a facilitator representing a higher education institution.

CHAPTER 7

Principal Isidro expressed his reflection pertaining to reciprocal learning as a team.

> I was interested in what I can learn from the university. I believe this is a two-way street. They're going to learn from us. But they've already been where we are right now. The university has challenged us. But without the help received from the university, I am not sure we would be where we are right now. I think this process has helped us to learn about each other, as well as from each other.

Inquiry Centered on Perceived Barriers

In this segment of inquiry, principals reflected on factors that could serve as barriers for advancing this work. They also spoke to the conditions they perceived as necessary for moving beyond the perceived barriers.

Existing Disconnect Between Post-Secondary Institutions and pK-12 School Districts

A reoccurring theme centered on the inquiry of perceived barriers was the perceived disconnect that exists between higher education and pK-12 school districts. The theme of barriers was described in several ways.

Disconnect Between Theory and Practice

Principal Edward reflected on the topic of barriers as it pertained to professors who have not practiced as a principal, or who have not practiced in many years.

> I think that the practices in higher education are going to have to change a little bit. I am talking about the "trap that professors of preparation programs get themselves into." A professor may say, "You know what, I was in a building. I was a building administrator." And I respond, great, "How long ago was that?" "Oh, it was 24 years ago." My response was, "I have been at this for 13 years," and "practice has changed significantly" in the last five years.

Principal Edward was referring to the significant change in role expectations for the principal. As expounded on in Chapters 1 and 2, the literature provided extensive evidence to support the changed role of the principal; from building manager, to that of instructional leader.

Principal Edward continued to speak to this disconnect as a perceived barrier that could impede the replication of this effort on a large-scale.

> This barrier continues to drive me crazy. In my conversations with some professors, they tell me that they are not going to go back and learn how PLCs work, because I have "already done that." But they cannot speak to PLCs because they have not been involved with them.

Principal Edward continued his reflection:

> And I do not mean to suggest that I am better because I am in the schools. I just mean to convey that many professors are disconnected with what is happening in our schools today. There seems to be a huge disconnect with most professors, as to what is happening in our buildings.

University Facilitator as an Outsider

Principal Edward mentioned a potential barrier, regarding a facilitator who represents the university. This barrier involved the limited knowledge that a university facilitator may have pertaining to district culture, issues, and needs. He also shared that depending upon individual qualities inherent to the facilitator this barrier has the potential of being worked through.

> One of the issues that took time to overcome, one of the things that we all felt like, or at least I did, was that "she's still an outsider." I was concerned that she didn't understand what was going on in our district.

As he continued his reflection, Principal Edward expounded on the process that helped to change what he perceived as a barrier between the district and the university.

> This issue has changed as well. She takes time to listen. She takes time to figure out what is going on. And even though she still may not completely understand, she does not pretend that she does.

Within the context of Principal Edward's final comments on this perceived barrier, the tenet of developing interdependent relationships and having the ability to place ones-self as learner and expert, served to minimize the impact of this perception.

Principal Edward used the following expression:

> She does not act like the savior of the world. If she does not understand something, she asks for clarification. She does not mind learning from us. She respects our answers and knowledge. I believe many professors from higher education believe they are the experts and the "saviors of the world."

Commitment

Principal Natalia brought to light the tenet of commitment. She asserted that the absence of a commitment from the university, will serve as a barrier, "Honestly, I cannot think of many barriers, specifically as this person is so committed. If she were not committed, it would definitely serve as a barrier."

Principal Natalia expounded upon her reflection centered on the potential barrier of commitment. Embedded in her reflection, were the additional tenets that she perceived as necessary for facilitating the effectiveness of this partnership.

This person meets with us every couple of weeks. We have a schedule for the year which guides our meeting times. We have the support from our administration. All central office administrators are included in the Administrators' PLC. Everybody's working in our PLC, and at the PLCs in their schools.

Access

The issue of access was presented in several ways, reflecting the perspectives of the principal participants.

Principal Natalia spoke to the issue of access as it pertained to the distance required for the university facilitator to travel:

> The only barrier that I can see is that the facilitator does not live here, and she's not readily available. She lives over two hours away. But she is really good about returning phone calls and responding to e-mails. So with this person, it is not a barrier, other that she's not right here within our district all of the time.

Principal Savannah reflected on the issue of access from a different lens. She address the potential issues of rural districts not having access to the resources generally provided by universities, "Some districts are fortunate to be located in cities where there is a college or university. But this is not the situation for all districts, especially rural districts."

As Principal Savannah expounded upon her reflection centered on issues of access, additional factors were brought to the forefront.

> Distance between a university and school district can increase the time involved in delivering services, the difficulty of bringing people together, and the increased cost involved in bringing people to rural districts.

Embedded in this discussion, was the possibility of resistance that could be present within the context of institutions of higher learning.

> I would hope that post-secondary institutions, especially colleges of education, would not feel resistant to providing support to rural districts, in light of the challenges. "We're all in the same business." I hope that those folks would be willing to participate with public schools, specifically rural schools.

Fiscal Limitations

Principal Isidro reflected on the potential barrier centered on limitations imposed by fiscal budgets.

> I can see monetary limitations arise, if we were paying for this. This would definitely pose a barrier. The university is working under a grant. When the grant runs out, this is likely to be a barrier.

Principal Isidro also addressed the factor of time-constraints, which could serve as a barrier to the sustainability of the partnership, "There could be time constraints for that person. Therefore, the person representing the university would understand the level of commitment."

Considering the expressed limitations which could serve as barriers, Principal Isidro expressed his preference regarding the partnership between the university and school district.

> Personally, I would prefer to have a partnership with the university. The university has access to the "teachers of teachers. And this is important to me." While I am no longer taking classes at the university, I like being around those people. I like to pick their brains.

INQUIRY CENTERED ON CONTINUOUS IMPROVEMENT EFFORTS

The final segment of inquiry highlighted the insights gleaned from the principal participants, centered on the conditions that could facilitate continuous improvement efforts between the university and district partnership. New themes emerged, as well as reoccurring themes that were highlighted in the first two segments of inquiry. Reoccurring themes involved factors of trust, access, and availability.

Trust and Access to Facilitators in the Partnerships

Principal Isidro reflected on two partnerships that are associated with the district from the university. As he reflected on the factors of trust, access, and availability, the term partnership was used interchangeably.

> We have on-going relationships between the university and district, providing services in different capacities. I really like the relationship we have with the two separate groups right now. I feel that I can call them after hours, if needed. I can e-mail them, text them, and obtain information that I need.

Principal Isidro expressed his desire for this level of interaction and accessibility to continue.

> I would want this level of availability to continue. From my view, my relationship with these two groups goes beyond their availability during their scheduled visits. My relationship with them involves accessibility and interaction. I enjoy interacting with them.

New themes which emerged in this segment included: the ability to take ownership of the partnership; sustainability; and support continuous improvement through the continuation of the Administrators' PLC platform.

CHAPTER 7

Ownership

Principal Kurtis provided his reflection pertaining to the need to take ownership of the Administrators' PLC after the involvement with the university comes to a close. As he provided his reflection regarding taking ownership of this process, he incorporated the related factors of sustainability and replicability.

> From my perspective, one of the nicest features about this whole process is that it is something that does not cost a lot of money. The biggest hurdle to overcome regarding sustainability is that when a grant ends, and the money goes away, the program usually goes away as well.

Principal Kurtis made the distinction between a program requiring considerable funding support and the Administrators' PLC, which from his viewpoint, does not. "We are putting a system into place that can continue and be replicated almost anywhere, because there aren't financial barriers."
Principal Kurtis continued his reflection:

> Not to simplify the process, as it has been complex, it really does involve people who are capable and willing to sit down and learn together, and talk about instruction for increasing student outcomes. I think this process should be happening in education much more than it does.

Principal Kurtis added: "This process has been very effective for us. Based on my own personal opinion, I would like to see this type and level of support available to other schools who struggle with this."
Principal Kurtis emphasized the specific importance of providing this level of support to rural districts.

> Because of the nature of our area, we have so many small rural districts. Within these districts, there may only be one or two or three administrators for any particular district. Perhaps through the incorporation of technology, these small districts can work together to form one Administrators' PLC.

Principal Isidro provided his insights on taking ownership of the Administrators' PLC.

> From my perspective, an indication of success means that you can let go. What I mean by letting go, is that as instructional leaders in the district, it is time to let go of the instructional leader from the university.

Principal Isidro reflected on the transition that is occurring in the district. The facilitator has increasingly provided opportunities for the associate superintendent and principal participants to facilitate the Administrators' PLC. "She has already started to do this. She is letting go more and more. As administrators, we are now taking turns to facilitate the Administrators' PLC."

between stakeholders within the context of a Professional Learning Community has significant importance. As the facilitator, I adhered to the principles associated with building leadership capacity in the context of job-embedded professional development with principals. In adherence to the principles, I felt it was of essence to operationalize the practice of interdependence. My intentional practice of placing myself as a learner as well as expert served to model the critical tenet of interdependence. I perceived it essential that the principals felt that they could contribute to the learning process, as they shared their specific areas of expertise. It was also quintessential for the participants to understand that I valued continuous learning. They needed to observe that I did not have the need to have expert knowledge in every area.

One way that I authentically demonstrated my need to continuously learn, was through my participation in trainings that directly affected pK-12, and our continuous improvement process. Over the years, I have attended district-wide trainings as well as trainings provided to the principals. Examples of these types of professional development included: the use of walk-through tools integrating technology, workshops on RtI, and district-wide workshops which involved a presenter from Solution Tree, to follow through on the learning experiences gleaned from attending the Professional Learning Communities Institute. In response to nationwide and state initiatives, my most recent training involved attending a three-day workshop centered on the Common Core Standards.

An integral goal from the trainings received was to integrate the learning to our identified outcomes, supported by our conceptual framework. I needed to ensure that the learning received by the participants did not result in a fragmented learning experience. As we developed throughout the years, collecting evidence that "we were doing what we set out to do," became increasingly critical to measure impact of our continuous improvement efforts. Therefore, working with the principal participants, we strived to integrate the learning into our practice. From my assessment, this is an area that warrants continued efforts centered on tenets of intentional practice and using data to inform our practice.

The line of inquiry centered on understanding the connection between the learning of the participants and the involvement of the university, brought to light several themes. As the themes were analyzed, it was determined that these themes were more appropriately classified under the category of "conditions." It was interpreted that there are several non-negotiable and negotiable conditions that need to be met and sustained, if the partnership is to realize the intended outcomes. The understanding of the necessary presence of these "conditions," brings to light the complexity and tenuousness entailed in facilitating second-order change efforts. These variable conditions reinforce the literature that speaks to the complexity of systemic change, which was expounded on in Chapters 1 and 2.

These conditions also reflect many of the elements found in effective PLCs, and in PLCs that can facilitate a paradigm-shift in thinking and in practice. Finally, the voices of the principals served to provide additional support for engaging in sustained job-embedded professional development. Such efforts can bring about the necessary paradigm shift that can make a difference in changing teacher behaviors for increasing student learning outcomes. These findings also support that this process is complex, and does not occur readily. The implications that these findings have for informing future practice, is discussed in the final chapter.

CONCLUSION

Chapter 7 explored the perceptions of the principal participants as it concerned the sustained effort of the university-district partnership. In this chapter, the principals communicated their insights concerning their involvement with the university, which endeavored to build leadership capacity through the development and implementation of the Administrators' PLC. The principals shared their individual and collective understandings pertaining to the outcomes of their individual and collective experiences.

This chapter was organized around three areas of inquiry. The intent was to provide a deeper understanding of the participants' perceptions centered on receiving job-embedded professional development provided through the sustained efforts of a university-district partnership. The three areas of inquiry were: receiving professional development from the partnership which involved a facilitator representing a higher education institution; perceived barriers; and recommendations for continuous improvement. Within the scope of this inquiry, several themes emerged, which have been analyzed and discussed in depth. This chapter concluded with interpretive analyses on the findings found within the emergent themes.

The final chapter synthesized the findings as they connected to further understanding the problem. Within the context of the analyses, specific implications were discerned. These implications facilitated recommendations as they aligned with the implications derived from the analyses. The recommendations were intended to speak to the members of the university community, researchers, school-districts, and policy-makers. These separate yet interdependent constituencies each play an integral role for informing the changing direction of education.

CHAPTER 8

NARRATIVE FROM THE LENS OF THE AUTHOR: A COMPELLING PURPOSE FOR THIS PROJECT

EXPERIENCE AS A PRINCIPAL FACILITATING SCHOOL IMPROVEMENT EFFORTS

I was a former principal who wore shoes that were much too large. I spent long waking hours walking in those uncomfortable shoes, consumed by the demands of the job. At times, I sauntered aimlessly in those shoes as I struggled to make sense of the chaos that went hand-in hand with implementing school improvement efforts that were both unwelcomed and misunderstood. I recalled the sleepless nights, enveloped with feelings of uncertainty, overwhelmed with the magnitude of my charge. Compelled to make a difference in teaching and in learning outcomes, I knew that I had to transform the existing culture of my school. I questioned whether I could realistically fill the looming gaps ever present in my shoes.

Having deep philosophical roots grounded in principles of constructivism, transformational leadership, humanistic leadership, servant leadership, developmental psychology, and Rogerian principles, I believed deeply in the ability to develop human potential. Later, I used language borrowed from the educational literature, which highlighted the idea of building leadership capacity. These principles became my beliefs of conviction. These concepts served to guide my practice, and influence my leadership lens. Unquestionably, these foundational systems were the cornerstone from which I approached the school improvement process.

Our school district was proud of the long-standing traditions and norms that comprised the culture of the high-school district, reflective of the community. Our once rural community was rapidly becoming urbanized. My high school was one of three high schools in the district; the oldest high-school most bound by traditions and age-old practices. During the rapid urbanization of our community, the district was fervently involved with the building of two new high schools.

My student population reached beyond capacity, to nearly 2,600 students. My school operated under a pervasive cloud of school reform. Confusion, chaos, uneasiness, mistrust, and resistance permeated the school climate. The district, not having a comprehensive understanding of the magnitude of the effects of deep second-order change, did put forth an effort to comply with mandated state and federal reforms.

One mechanism which was put into place was a district study group. This group was facilitated by the associate superintendent of curriculum and instruction, and required the attendance of the site-based principals. His leadership style was overbearingly authoritative. He enlisted distrust as the principals and teachers were aware of his self-serving and often punitive agenda, masked by a congenial demeanor. He often invited stakeholders to communicate honestly. After brief encounters with him, it was common knowledge that consequences would be incurred for not sharing a similar perspective, or for partaking in honest disclosure.

We were provided with books to read, and encouraged to engage in discussions. However, apprehension, competiveness, mistrust, favoritism, and self-serving practices permeated the air of the existing climate. This atmosphere made it nearly impossible for the team to emerge as a cohesive group, grounded by a collective sense of purpose. We were principals who did not form strong collegial bonds with one another. We were superficially congenial. We went through the motions of compliance during district-wide meetings. Upon return to our respective school-sites, we waddled in our uncomfortable shoes of different sizes, perpetuating the cultural norm of isolated practices, distrust, and competitiveness. For reasons I can no longer recall, the study group was dismantled. The practice of implementation and dismantling of programs was also reflective of our culture norm.

I was charged with leading a comprehensive high school, challenged with the complexity of a swiftly changing landscape. Our assistant principals, and most of our teachers, were long-time veterans of the school. Many still lived in the community or nearby communities. Teachers and the administrative team perplexed by the rapid wave of change often took refuge by engaging in the sharing of stories. They reminisced of "how things used to be." Many of the faculty were experiencing a sense of loss, which is frequently an effect of second-order change. Their sense of loss, acted out in various ways, was not initially understood or supported.

During that time, my school had been identified as a school in corrective action. I can now light-heartedly reflect on the experience where my colleague of the "newer" and "better" school, used me, my teachers, and my school as an example of what not to become. I was attending a meeting with his high-school department heads. In the midst of the principal's conversation to his department-heads, he said, "we never want to become like her school."

Paradoxically, with the unwavering support and work of my once recalcitrant teachers, my school later outperformed his school on standardized tests. This unexpected outcome served as one prong to challenge previously held assumptions about the effectiveness of my leadership and the capacity of my teachers.

The effects of second-order change in my school served to realize overarching ideas, supported by the educational change literature. Deep, second-order change efforts created confusion and chaos, as long-standing assumptions were both questioned and challenged. The sense of order that once was, is no longer present. The coveted sense of stability maintained by the status-quo has now been shaken.

Over time, my school had made significant changes evidenced by our eventual commitment to embrace and engage in the school improvement process. Trustingly, I operated under the assumption that the district would be pleased with the changes that I was able to facilitate with my hard-working faculty, who increasingly shared a common purpose. The impact of second-order change created an unexpected outcome. From my lens, the more efficacious I became with implementing and embedding the tenets of second-order change, the more apprehensive the central office administrators became.

From my interpretation, I believed that they did not want negative consequences to occur for my school, since we were a school in corrective action. However, I realized that the central office administrators were not prepared at many levels, for my school, or for me, to experience successes that were not initially associated with that school. The successes were reserved for the other two schools. This assumption was never verbalized. However, it was powerfully permeated in the decisions which were made and through the attitudes which were conveyed.

In due course, my teachers and I became more comfortable with the change process. We saw evidence of improvement indicated by changed teacher behaviors; increased teacher ownership; ability to arrive at decision-making consensus as it connected to student outcomes; increased understanding of the role of data; increased teacher and student attendance; and gains on standardized tests. These examples provided indication that we were progressing through our school improvement journey.

As I had gained increasing support from my teachers, as well as evidence that we were moving the school in a healthier direction, my priorities began to shift. I was now able to shift my attention on issues that would facilitate the sustainability of the efforts put forth from my teachers, administrative team, students and members of the community. I began to make different requests than I had previously.

I now wanted and needed control of my school budget. Part of time-honored traditions and practices reflective of my school was our football team. I was the only school in the district whose school budget was operated by the assistant principal of athletics. Another request was that I wanted to sustain the DuFour model of PLCs in my school. Ironically, the district was principally very supportive of the implementation of this model, to facilitate the school improvement process.

Initially, the two other high-schools were invited to partake in this model. When both schools declined to implement this model at their schools, I was still permitted to maintain the model. However, once the model took a threshold in the school, I felt the resistance from central office. From my lens, implementing the model to meet state mandated initiatives was acceptable. However, embracing the model that served to facilitate a cultural shift and actuate second-order change, proved to be controversial.

The district was not prepared with the tidal wave of systemic change implications that were embedded in reform models and mandated state initiatives. They also did not realize that the implementation of a Professional Learning Community (PLC) as the selected model to facilitate school reform and improvement would create a platform for challenging their assumptions, existing norms, and long-standing practices. It was not possible for them to foresee the multifaceted implications. In reflection, I am uncertain as to whether the stakeholders representing central office would have equated their complicated experience with the systemic change process.

CHAPTER 8

REFLECTING ON LESSONS LEARNED

This pivotal and transformational experience has been invaluable. This experience has served to reinforce certain assumptions, while challenging others. I approached the treacherous school reform process from the lens of the theoretical frameworks that have shaped me as a principal. My practice today as a professor has been truly informed by the many lessons learned. I was grateful for this attained development, realized from this experience of having been a principal who never was able to grow into the shoes I wore.

Having had first-hand experience with the change process as a principal, the work of Robert Evans had specific resonance as it connected to my leadership lens. In Evan's work on the *Human Side of School Change*, he eloquently synthesized his position regarding the school change process:

> School change requires a belief in the potential for improving people, but it also requires an acceptance—a love—of people as they are. To truly accomplish all that we can, we must hold fast to the core commitments that give life and education promise—but we must also appreciate what constitutes genuine progress toward our goals. Real change is always personal; organizational change is always incremental. In the best of schools, with the best resources and the most skillful leadership, the time frame for transforming culture, structure, belief, and practice is years. Success will require the highest strivings and the most down-to-earth expectations. Only if we maintain a healthy respect for the lessons of experience can real hope truly triumph. (cited in Evans, 2001, p. 299)

Another significant lesson learned from this experience and also supported by Evans and other researchers is that deep change takes time. It is not magical. Rather it is multidimensional, comprehensive, complex, and all-consuming. This level of change requires the placement of several conditions which have been discussed throughout this book and brought to light in the findings by the principal participants of the 5-year university-district partnership. Deep change affecting people is always tenuous, and sometimes precarious. Change promises to unsteady the status-quo, and create chaos of what once was a seemingly stable environment.

THE FIVE-YEAR UNIVERSITY-DISTRICT PARTNERSHIP

As a researcher and facilitator who participated in this partnership, the portrayal of my theoretical frameworks, experiences, and assumptions, certainly have played an influential role in my momentum to partake in the 5-year university-district partnership. This lens also served to reinforce the dissonance I experienced in partaking in the delivery of well-intended, yet fragmented professional development efforts provided to school districts. I understood that not all types of professional development require second-order change efforts. However, I operated under the premise that most of our professional development efforts should not be spent on programmatic initiatives that provided little evidence of changing teaching and learning outcomes. This assumption had resonance for me, specifically when many of the schools in districts we worked with, were not meeting Adequate Yearly Progress. An outcome of not meeting AYP led to being identified as Schools in Need of Improvement (SINOI).

With several decades spanning school reform efforts, engaging in whole-school reform has become what I have referred to as the cultural norm. The era of perpetual accountability, influenced by educational leadership literature and educational policy, have served to change how we conceptualize the role of the principal. New expectations, undoubtedly, were associated with the changing role of the principal. Brought to light by the literature embedded in the early chapters of this book, the principal is now expected to think and perform as an instructional leader. The instructional leader is now expected to facilitate job-embedded learning communities for teachers which hold promise of changing teacher behaviors that can make a difference in learning outcomes for our students. An inherent gap lies between what is expected of today's principal, and the aligned supports offered throughout the pK-20 pipeline.

The presence of the aforementioned disconnected practices propelled me to further the exploration of what I felt was an under-researched topic. Much of the focus of school improvement efforts had been placed on developing teacher capacity. One vehicle for accomplishing this objective was through the delivery of job-embedded learning opportunities through the implementation of teachers' PLCs. Principals, who were increasingly perceived as instructional leaders, were charged with the facilitation and oversight of these PLCs. I perceived the wide implementation of teachers' PLCs intended to change teacher behaviors, facilitated by many principals who have not experienced this initiative, served as a disconnected practice.

In light of the increased expectations placed on today's principals, much less focus was targeted to provide sustained job-embedded professional development for principals. I held the assumption that principals required additional support and development which spanned the scope of their principal preparation programs. This had a specific bearing for principals who have been seated for several years, prior to the curricular changes and changes in practice which were made and continue to be made in university preparation programs.

When provided with the opportunity to provide outreach and professional development services to districts affiliated with the Alliance, I became concerned with the programmatic delivery efforts provided to districts. I perceived that these well-intended delivery formats served to unintentionally perpetuate disconnected practices. Most of these districts had SINOI designations. Therefore, these districts and schools were in need of a systemic approach that addressed second-order change principles.

The collaboration between the university and the Southwest School District eventually developed into a partnership as brought to light in the literature in the earlier chapters of this book. The sustained partnership efforts provided the opportunity to develop a platform in which to explore the ways that principals may perceive and respond to sustained job-embedded professional development which was centered on building leadership capacity.

CHAPTER 8

PRESENTATION AND SYNTHESIS OF FINDINGS

The remainder of this chapter focused on providing a presentation and synthesis of the findings, which propelled a discussion derived from the findings. A brief depiction of changes made in how school year progress is now measured, has been provided. A chart reflecting the grades for the Southwest School District provides the reader with a snapshot of the indicators that facilitate a school grade. Presentation of descriptive data depicting district trends has also been provided. The presentation of this data was intended to provide a complete picture of the findings, gleaned from the principals and participants who engaged in this 5-year project. A discussion on the implications derived from the findings was brought to light, which informed the recommendations provided.

A-B-C-D-F SCHOOL GRADING SYSTEM 2011

The recent response by our state to address the "moving target" of changing accountability criteria is suggestive that the era of accountability has become the cultural norm for most school districts and states. New Mexico has 122 school districts and 831 schools. As depicted by Figure 1, 719 schools, or 87% of the schools in New Mexico did not meet Adequate Yearly Progress in 2010–2011. Only 112 of the 831 schools, which comprised 13% of the schools, met AYP criteria.

School grading is part of a state and federal statute that mandates accountability for all schools (NMPED, 2012, retrieved from www.ped.state.nm.us). The Elementary and Secondary Education Act (ESEA) enacted in 1965, which was reauthorized in 2001 as *No Child Left Behind* (NCLB), requires schools to demonstrate annual improvement in mathematics and in reading. In 2011, New Mexico Lawmakers enacted additional requirements that schools demonstrate progress through a grading system similar to that applied to students, A-B-C-D-F [6.19.8.1 NMAC–N, 12-15-11] (NMPED, 2012, retrieved from www.ped.state.nm.us)

An intended outcome of using the A-B-C-D-F school grading system is that partial credit is provided for all indicators (NMPED, 2012, retrieved from www.ped.state.nm.us). Using AYP criteria, targets must be met by schools in an "all-or-none" fashion in order to receive any credit. Therefore, a school that scored near the threshold was treated no differently than a school that significantly missed the mark.

Highlighted in the NPED report (2012), retrieved from www.ped.state.nm.us, 87% of our schools failed to meet the targets. The report underscored that the goal of accountability is to assist in the reform of poorly performing schools, while highlighting the methods of successful schools. Hence, the AYP model was too limited to inform this process. The recently implemented grading system contains a rich set of feedback indicators intended to assist schools to identify weak areas, plan, and improve (NMPED, 2012, retrieved from www.ped.state.nm.us).

NARRATIVE FROM THE LENS OF THE AUTHOR

Table 1. *Report Card for Southwest School District—reflecting grading system*

Southwest School District								
Schools	AYP-Met	AYP-Not	Overall Grade	Status	School	Highest 75%	Lowest 75%	Other Academic Indicators
Elementary School 1		1	C	B	D	F	D	A
Elementary School 2		1	C	B	B	C	F	A
Elementary School 3	1		A	A	A	C	A	A
Elementary School 4	1		C	C	F	F	D	A
Middle School		1	C	D	D	C	C	A
High School		1	C	B	NA	D	F	A

PRESENTATION OF DESCRIPTIVE DATA—SCALED SCORES OF THE SOUTHWEST SCHOOL DISTRICT

Figure 2 is a representation of the mean scaled scores between 2008 and 2012 for the six schools in the Southwest School District. A mean per year for each school was created to locate the total mean for the district. The data depicted in this graph described trend data, before the model of the Administrators' PLC was commenced and after the implementation of the model for three years. The collaboration was emergent in 2008 and the Administrators' PLC was implemented in the fall semester of 2009.

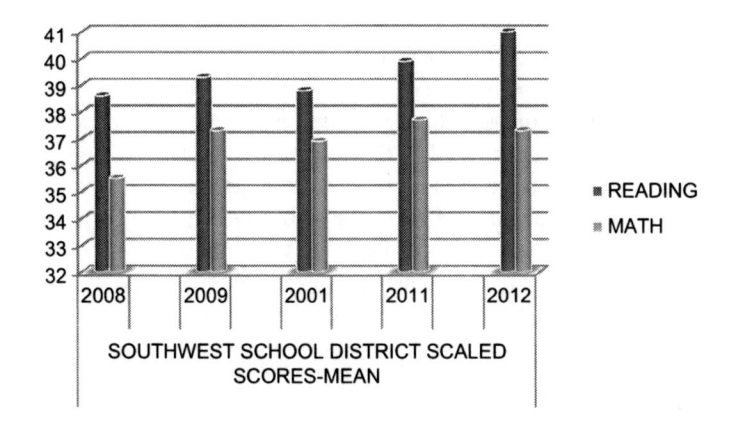

Figure 2. Southwest District mean scaled scores: 2008–2009.

CHAPTER 8

DISCUSSION OF IMPLICATIONS DERIVED FROM THE FINDINGS

The findings from the principals' voices and all stakeholders who participated in the Administrators' PLC, suggested that significant outcomes associated with participants' growth were realized. Most of the participants felt that this growth had served to change their practice at their respective sites. Reflective of the AYP data, the changed system of the use of the School Report Card, and the scaled scores presented in the trend data it may be injudicious to make a direct correlation between principals' growth and the impact on student achievement.

Several emergent themes were brought to light in the findings chapters, which were analyzed in-depth, utilizing an interpretive case study approach. In this final chapter, a concerted focus was to expound on the implications of specific themes that have a particular bearing on informing future practice, research, and policy.

DISCUSSION ON REPLICABILITY

The inquiry of whether and to the extent that this model of providing job-embedded professional development focused on principals, can be replicated, has been the center of many discussions with the participants. I have approached this discussion from three different perspectives. I have first discussed the issue of replicability from the participants' lens. Second, I have addressed the issue of replicability from my lens, looking at this issue from the lens of a professor and researcher, who facilitated the Administrators' PLCs. Third; I have strived to integrate both perspectives as it pertained to this topic.

Overtime, the principal participants did find relevance of having received sustained job-embedded professional development. The participants found that they were able to utilize many of the tenets learned in the Administrators' PLCs, and put into applicable practice. Most of the participants who received individual coaching also reported that this experience was valuable for supporting their practice.

As administrators, they were charged with implementing an already existing model of PLCs for teachers at their respective sites. They were also charged with the outcomes of the implementation of this model. From their lens, the PLC model for teachers has been replicated throughout the nation, as its practice has gained increased acceptance. The model of PLCs, specifically the DuFour model of PLCs, is increasingly implemented in school districts throughout New Mexico. Many of the schools who have not made AYP, or have received a SINOI designation are implementing this model as a means to facilitate school improvement efforts.

From their lens, most of all participants expressed the need to continue the Administrators' PLC as it connected to supporting the continuous improvement process.

> At this point in time, I think continuing this process is very important. I believe that when we meet, we remain intentional about continuous improvement. We have to keep asking, "what can we do to improve?" Especially with changes that affect us, like the Common Core Standards.

NARRATIVE FROM THE LENS OF THE AUTHOR

Several of the participants in the Administrators' PLC concurred with the assertion made by Principal Kuris, as he addressed the issue of replication. Principal Kurtis embedded several conditions into his reflection, which were at the center of discussions with the principal participants on several occasions. These conditions or provisions highlighted the complexity of the process. It can be implied that if the complexity of the process and the criteria required for effective implementation are not met, the implementation process and prospect of sustainability, could be hindered. "We are putting a system into place that can continue and be replicated almost anywhere, because there aren't financial barriers." He continued,

> Not to simplify the process, as it has been complex, it really does involve people who are capable and willing to sit down and learn together, and talk about instruction for increasing student outcomes. I think this process should be happening in education much more than it does.

From this viewpoint, replication had more to do with attaining an understanding and commitment between the central office administrators and the university, who would be implementing and facilitating the PLC. Fewer participants felt that this model could be implemented with a facilitator not associated with a university. Factors of access, affordability, feasibility, credibility, and the willingness of a facilitator not associated with the university to partner with a district were brought to light by the majority of the participants.

REPLICABILITY FROM MY LENS AS THE UNIVERSITY FACILITATOR

A reoccurring theme threaded in the findings, was the theme of necessary conditions or provisions. The presence of necessary conditions was directly connected to the perceived effectiveness and sustainability of the partnership which delivered the job-embedded professional development through the model of the Administrators' PLC.

The principal participants spoke to the necessary conditions inherent to team building and relationship building which were reoccurring themes highlighted in the findings. Factors of safety, trust, and the establishment of a sense of comfort were unequivocally necessary conditions, if the principals were to take necessary risks and engage in purposeful conversations. The conditions of relevance, knowledge, and credibility, as it pertained to the university facilitator, were of essence. The principals felt that my former experience as a secondary principal, who was involved deeply in school improvement efforts, was a necessary criterion for earning credibility and gaining trust.

This finding had paradoxical implications. On the one hand, the principals looked up to the university as the purveyors of knowledge. This perception had specific bearing, as the participants felt that the university played a paramount role in research, as well as in the preparation of prospective teachers and principals. Therefore, it was perceived

CHAPTER 8

that the university was responsible for ensuring that school districts had access to current best-practices in the field. Second, the findings suggested that the university had a responsibility to support principals' job-embedded professional development and learning that spans the scope of their university preparation programs.

The enigma herein lies: On the other hand, most principal participants in this 5-year project conveyed their concerns about professors' outdated practical knowledge and over-reliance on the teaching of theory. A condition that was underscored by the participants is that the partners from the university should have relevant experience as a former school administrator. This condition in and of itself was not sufficient to gain the principals' trust. This condition alone was also not sufficient for addressing the relevance of the professional development. However, the participants emphatically conveyed the importance that the university facilitator "knew what it was like to walk in their shoes."

Continuing this discussion on replicability from my lens, it must be taken into consideration that this 5-year project was a bound case study employed to gain an in-depth understanding of the situation and meaning for those involved (Merriam, 1998). As a researcher, I was more interested in discovery at this juncture, than in attaining confirmation (Merriam, 1998). I was focused on the ways that gleaning insights from this project can have a bearing on informing policy, practice, and future research (Merriam, 1998).

As a single case study, the researcher cannot be hasty in making generalizations, one factor that influences replicability. However, reader or user generalizability (Merriam, 1998) involved leaving the extent to which the findings in this study may apply to other schools. The depiction of the data provided in the graphs will help the reader to determine the degree of transferability or case-to-case transfer, as described by Firestone (1993 in Merriam, 1998).

Another issue of replicability from my lens as a researcher was centered on the under-researched area of providing job-embedded professional development for seated principals who have successfully completed principal and administration preparation programs. The research is abundant on the need for job-embedded professional development to occur for teachers. Incongruously, it is the principals who have been charged with the implementation, facilitation, and oversight of job-embedded professional development for teachers. Further, in the context of how the role of the 21st century principal is perceived today, principals are increasingly held responsible for providing evidence that correlates teacher job-embedded development and improved student learning outcomes.

From my perspective, the pre-requisite condition of attaining consensus by the educational community, which includes researchers and policymakers, precedes the discussion on replicability of this model. Critical conversations centered on determining the commitment to employ a systemic effort to further explore the gap which exists between role expectations and sustained support is of precedence. The literature provided indication that the role of the 21st century is markedly different than in recent history.

As an educational community, we have not significantly changed our viewpoints and practices which support principals beyond their preparation programs. This shift in thinking and in practice may be necessary for helping principals to build upon their individual and collective capacities, in an effort to increase the impact of implemented whole-school reform models. Subsequent research which pursues to expand the scope of this study to reach a larger number of diverse constituents, will serve to provide further insight intended to inform the next steps.

Another condition was centered on the acknowledgement that most whole-school reform models are associated with second-order change principles. Therefore, a systemic approach to whole-school reform must be considered. From my collective experiences, I have operated under the assumption that this tenet is widely misunderstood, and therefore not widely supported.

DISCUSSION ON REPLICABILITY FROM AN INTEGRATIVE APPROACH

I have attempted to consider the complex issue of replicability from the lens of the participants. I also explored this issue from my perspective, operating from the lens of a researcher. The participants, serving as school leaders, provided a divergent perspective on replicability, as they considered factors pertinent to school leaders who are charged with the operational challenges of leading their schools. From my lens, it was imperative that I considered the research principles in adherence to how I approached the study. Consequently, the paradigms would be different. The integration of tenets reflective of both paradigms, could provide insight to how further studies are approached.

DISCUSSION ON CAPACITY

Principal Kurtis also spoke to the issue of capability of the stakeholders. I referred to this tenet as capacity of stakeholders, which is a required tenet needed to develop and sustain interdependent relationships that comprise a collaborative setting. From my experience, I believe the critical tenet of understanding the integral role that capacity plays in collaborative settings is underestimated.

It is to be expected that varying levels of capacity will be evidenced between stakeholders. This observation will be particularly apparent at the commencement of a collaborative effort. However, different skills sets and attributes between stakeholders are not to be confused with the functioning level of a stakeholder in the collaboration. In essence, it is the ability of stakeholders to recognize, appreciate, and eventually depend on the different skill sets and contributions of other stakeholders, which facilitate the dynamics of interdependence (Rubin, 2002) within the collaboration. These efforts will contribute to the attainment of the collectively agreed upon outcomes to the degree and extent that the quality of interdependence can be cultivated and nurtured. This facet has implications for principals, as they build upon their capacity to help teachers in PLCs function as an interdependent group, bound together by a common purpose.

CHAPTER 8

The level of capacity as it refers to functioning levels of individual stakeholders has implications for all members within the collaboration. If the members are cognizant of attaining an interdependent group where the individual and collective contributions are maximized (Rubin, 2002), the need to build capacity of individual members is critical. This is not accomplished readily, easily, or even immediately. However, it must be recognized that levels of competency between members cannot remain significantly discrepant for prolonged periods of time (Rubin, 2002).

If one stakeholder's level of capacity is significantly lower than that of other members in the collaboration, and the learning curve is not bridged, the sustained gap is likely to create issues of mistrust and ambivalence (Rubin, 2002). Over time, members of the collaboration will grow weary of over-compensating for that stakeholder's lower level of capacity or performance, which does not support the changing and fluid needs of the collaboration. This dynamic could have a negative effect on the functioning level of the collaboration. It can also impact the willingness of other stakeholders to continue contributing to the group.

I have found this complex interplay to be present in teachers' PLCs, in our Administrators' PLC, as well as in various collaborative settings within the context of the university. I also felt that mechanisms within collaborations are not sufficiently in place to adequately address this critical dynamic which poses as a barrier for sustaining effective collaborations.

Another dimension of capacity pertains to the issue of human and fiscal resources. The findings indicated that most of the participants valued the coaching that was implemented in an effort to augment the work of the Administrators' PLC. However, this practice had to be discontinued due to limited resources. The issue of limited resources had several implications. Universities have opportunities to hire and support faculty who have more inclination to engage in sustained collaborative efforts with school districts. This issue has specific bearing for rural school districts who struggle with issues of access to nearby universities. The literature brought to light that rural districts face specific challenges pertaining to hiring of faculty to meet the diverse needs of the district.

DISCUSSION ON SUSTAINABILITY

Finally, in consensus with several of his colleagues, Principal Kurtis addressed the required condition of coming together and perhaps staying together, for the purpose of cultivating and sustaining a shared vision. The cultivation of a shared vision was the resilient thread that collectively kept the stakeholders together, bound by a cultivated sense of purpose. This thread bore specific importance, specifically as the collaboration or partnership encounters tensions, difficult situations, and the implementation dip, which Michael Fullan has addressed in his numerous publications. These dynamics are inherent to complex systems. Even a seemingly benign collaboration of four or five teachers, comprises the complex dynamics found in larger organizational systems.

As of this writing, the university-district partnership is approaching the end of its fifth year. The findings and perspectives pertaining to the issue of sustainability differed between participants. Several participants felt that it was important to take ownership of the PLC, and continue the work after the university involvement ceases. Some participants expressed their interest in continuing the work with the university.

Principal Isidro offered his perception on the need for the district to take full ownership of the process:

> From my perspective, an indication of success means that you can let go. What I mean by letting go, is that as instructional leaders in the district, it is time to let go of the instructional leader from the university.

Principal Isidro provided his insights to the steps being taken in order for this transition to occur. "She has already started to do this. She is letting go more and more. As administrators, we are now taking turns to facilitate the Administrators' PLC."

Writing from the lens of the university facilitator, I shared the perspective of the administrators who felt they can continue the Administrators' PLC without indefinite structured support from the university. From my analysis and interpretation on this issue, I held the notion that there is a fine line between interdependence and dependence. To embrace this discussion, it is important to recall the underlying philosophy of job-embedded professional development. One of the underlying tenets is to build individual and collective capacity of the group as it connects to realizing the collectively desired outcome. Prolonged participation after the goals have been met may serve to hinder this objective.

An area of continued growth for the individual participants that comprised the Administrators' PLC, was for the members to increase their varying degrees of comfort level and skill in the facilitation of the Administrators' PLC. Another area that had implications for continued growth was the ability to implement, monitor, and assess the practices of the decisions made within the Administrators' PLC.

I am hopeful that the administrators who comprised the principals and central office administrators continue to enhance and develop this platform to meet the changing needs of the district and the respective school-sites. Most of the stakeholders valued the tenet of continuous improvement. The findings provided evidence that most of the participants have made connections between their individual and collective continuous improvement efforts and the need to support the continuous improvement process of their teachers. After the formal parting of the stakeholders that comprised the university-district partnership, it is my sincere inclination that the participants will continue to work together to build-upon the tenets we have cultivated in the five-year partnership.

> Despite the nationwide emphasis on school improvement, the complexities of accomplishing desired systemic changes have been given short shrift in policy research, training, and practice.
>
> Adelman and Taylor (2007)

CHAPTER 8

RECOMMENDATIONS

Research on systemic change conducted by Adelman and Taylor (2007) posited that change is of central importance as it connected with efforts to improve schools. A critical assertion that was made in their research, brought to light that too little attention has been paid to the complexities of implementation, as the nation's research agenda does not include major initiatives to delineate and test models for widespread replication of education reforms (Adelman & Taylor, 2007). The findings derived from participants' voices, which facilitated interpretive analyses that led to a discussion on implications, supported the overarching assertion made by Adelman and Taylor (2007). Three recommendations which were made in their research on addressing systemic change efforts are of specific relevance to this project.

1. Adelman and Taylor (2007) suggested the intensification to prioritize status of federal research related to understanding systemic change concerns involved in school improvement. An emphasis on building conceptual models and developing and evaluating specific interventions for dealing with the processes and problems associated with introducing, sustaining, and scaling-up new initiatives and reforms.
2. Policymakers should ensure that school improvement planning guides are expanded to include a section on how the improvements will be accomplished.
3. A portion of funds currently allocated for school improvement should be redeployed to underwrite the costs of developing staff for systemic change, especially training for change leadership and change agent staff.

ADDITIONAL RECOMMENDATIONS

1. Universities have made significant gains to partner with school districts to redesign and co-design principal preparation programs that authentically integrated the voices of the school districts. Universities have also embraced various state and federal initiatives that have facilitated comprehensive refinement and revitalization efforts in their respective preparation programs. This was highlighted in the work completed with the Senate Joint Memorial 3: 2008 initiative, described in Chapter 2.

   Regardless of on-going initiatives to improve the quality and effectiveness of principal preparation programs, it was the viewpoint of my university colleagues that university principal preparation programs serves as one critical piece of the equation for addressing school improvement efforts. We also proposed that realistic expectations are placed on university preparation programs, to include university preparation programs that have been authentically co-designed with school districts.

   In an era marked by accountability and rapid change, a case has been made in the early chapters of this book which underscored the benefits of collaboration. Inherent to the challenges universities and districts face in forming and in sustaining

partnerships, this type of collaboration is needed to address the complexities of supporting teachers and principals to change practices that can make a difference in student learning outcomes. Therefore, it is recommended that utilizing these partnerships can be a next step to address the co-design and implementation of delivering job-embedded professional development for teachers and principals.
2. Crucial conversations centered on determining the commitment to employ a systemic effort to further explore the gap which exists between changed role expectations for today's principals, and the types of sustained supports available to principals, need to be held across the pK-20 pipeline. Policymakers must be included in these efforts.
3. Additional research is needed that seeks to expound on the less-studied topic of how principals respond to receiving additional learning in a job-embedded context, that spans the scope of principal preparation programs.
4. Additional research that expands the number of participants, and reaches different constituents is recommended. This study focused on principals bound in a single-case study. Therefore, studies intended to hear the voices and present understandings of other principals in various settings; superintendents; and the voices of school-board members; is of particular relevance.

MY CONCLUDING REFLECTION

I have been very privileged to have had the sustained opportunity to work with very hard-working and dedicated school administrators. I have forged strong relationships that have enriched both my life and my practice. I have learned much from the experiences and perspectives of these steadfast administrators who are truly vested in attaining the best learning outcomes for the students whom they serve. I am grateful for my university and for the Alliance at the university, who supported my vision, and gave me "academic license" to explore an area that compelled me. Without the individual and collective efforts of both systems, the emergent collaboration would not have developed into a partnership, bound by a cultivated shared sense of purpose and vision.

I credited this experience for serving to keep my practical knowledge current, as I engaged in numerous professional development opportunities that the district graciously invited and supported my participation. My ability to integrate theoretical constructs with current best-practices in the field as they have contextual relevance, has served my graduate students well. My former experiences as a secondary principal have provided me with credibility in this project, and have assisted the integration of practice and theory in the teaching of my courses.

This sustained experience with the university-district partnership involving the regular work with school administrators, has served as a platform to keep my knowledge of initiatives and best practices that impact pK-12 schools, current. Most recent examples are centered on our work with the Common Core, the transition from AYP as a primary measurement for the use of school improvement to the use of School Report Cards, and the integration of technology to conduct school

CHAPTER 8

walkthroughs. From my lens, without the intentional conversations centered on the complex topic of school improvement as it connects to the role of today's principal, without the continuous "re-tooling" that has been afforded to me through this experience, I would run the risk of becoming a "sage on the stage." Our current and prospective school leaders in the 21st century are less tolerant of this pedantic and outmoded delivery of preparation.

From this lens of a researcher, I hold the responsibility of affirming the strengths of the project. I also have the responsibility to bring to light the inherent complexities and limitations of engaging in a partnership that contains multifaceted dimensions. The educational literature on university-district partnerships made a case for the need and benefits for universities and districts to form collaborative agreements. The literature also brought to light the inherent challenges that these two systems face, which can serve as a barrier for implementation and sustainability.

I would be remiss if I did not speak to these inherent challenges from a stakeholder who was appreciably vested in this partnership. First and foremost, partnerships are composed of people. It goes without saying that the human condition is complex and tenuous. The inherent challenges brought to light by the literature on university-district partnerships addressed factors of personality, values, personal agendas, resources, and capacity.

As a stakeholder, I have experienced each of these dynamics played out in various ways throughout the partnership. We were fortunate that we were able to cultivate and sustain a common sense of purpose during the early phases of the collaboration. Both partners worked diligently to keep this purpose at the forefront of our work. Sharing a common purpose centered on core beliefs as it pertained to attaining school outcomes, served to maintain an unwavering focus. I believed this principle has served to keep us together when the stakes were high.

One of the tenuous beliefs that need to be nurtured in this complex arrangement is the idea of institutional needs being met (Rubin, 2002). There have been times when the partners have not seen eye to eye. There have been occasions when the partners have experienced conflict and tension. There have been times when difficult conversations were broached; centered on changing priorities, varying agendas, and the perception that someone's needs in a specific context, were conceded or had not been met.

The literature on university and district partnerships brought to light the inherent differences that could facilitate tensions, which can lead to conflict. The literature brought to the surface that in some cases, unresolved tensions can lead to the premature dissolution of the partnership. Fortunately, premature dismantling of the partnership was not experienced in the case of this university-district partnership.

While my assessment may not be in congruence with all of the stakeholders, I have determined that the time has neared for the district to take full ownership of the Administrators' PLC and the continuous improvement process. It is time to take steps to put closure on what I have evaluated as a long and successful partnership, formed between two inherently different systems, brought together to fulfill a common purpose. Closure, is usually difficult as it signifies change. And change, as addressed earlier, can be equated with a sense of loss. From my lens, we have been fortunate to come together and stay together for a duration that has provided evidence of individual and collective growth for all stakeholders. The outcomes that have been realized over the span of five years may not have been attained without the combined efforts, resources, skills, and insights, brought together by two systems.

CLOSING PASSAGE

In closing, I have left the reader with the captivating sentiments of Douglas Reeves (2009). These sentiments resonated with the intrinsic forces which have inspired me to implement and write about this 5-year project.

I was captivated by Reeves' eloquent use of the jury as a metaphor to delineate the complex and frequently subjective process of decision making. Describing the intricate process of what a jury embraces when making a difficult and complex decision, Reeves, made the point that regardless of which reform initiative you may be pondering from the number of available reform initiatives, you need not to incessantly contemplate the question (Reeves, 2009).

> When a unanimous decision is required, such as in a criminal trial, even a single juror can prevent the other 11 jurors from reaching a conclusion. In some jurisdictions, for a civil case on 9 out of 12 jurors must come to a conclusion to resolve the case, thus allowing 4 of 12—only 33 percent—to stop the decision-making process in its tracks. Sometimes the jury is deadlocked because of a single person who is wracked by conscience and full of doubt, and we revere the character made famous by Henry Fonda in *Twelve Angry Men* for maintaining the position of his opposition. Other cases involve a single recalcitrant juror who ignores the evidence, injects personal bias, fears community reaction to an unpopular verdict, or disregards the conclusions of the majority of the jury for reasons having nothing to do with the evidence at hand. Sometimes the jurors are fearful of making a mistake, as either decision in a case will lead to an adverse consequence for someone. (p.144)

> When a jury is deadlocked, only two choices are available. The first is the so-called hung jury, a deliberative body that is unable to consider the evidence before it and come to a conclusion. The second and most common choice is for the judge to instruct the jurors to continue to deliberate, try again, examine the evidence, use their own skills and abilities, work harder, and then come to a conclusion. In the vast majority of cases, their hard work pays off, the jurors work longer, reason through the evidence, consider multiple points of view, and ultimately follow their duty to make a decision based on the best evidence they have available. What the jury is never permitted to do is to simply wait endlessly in the jury room until perfect evidence arrives. They must render a decision based on the evidence at hand. (pp. 144–145)

CHAPTER 8

Through the utilization of the jury metaphor, Reeves made the powerful connection to the ongoing debates within the context of our complex educational system.

> In many education debates, we must now decide whether we as teachers, leaders, policymakers and citizens shall be a hung jury, waiting for evidentiary perfection as another generation of students fails to receive improved opportunities. (p.146)

Concluding with his use of the metaphor of the hung jury, he asserted that as an educational community, we have our choice of mistakes (Reeves, 2009).

> At the conclusion of your deliberations, members of the jury, you do not have a choice of perfection. Rather, you must choose one of two mistakes. The first mistake is that you will enact vital educational changes even though they will sometimes be ineffective and unnecessary. Having made this mistake, you will suffer the criticisms of cynics who, a year later say, "See, I told you we didn't need that!" (pp. 145–146).

Reeves described the second mistake:

> The second mistake is that you fail to enact vital educational changes, and another year, two years—perhaps a generation—will pass before someone else will use the same information that you had and will, at last, enact the changes you considered. Leaders at every level, along with a generation of students, will at that time ask, "Why didn't you do this earlier?" (p.146).

Reeves posed the final question: "The final question therefore is not 'How do we make perfect decisions?' Rather, the essential question is 'How do we choose the wiser mistake to make?'" (p. 146)

In light of the complex educational landscape of the 21st century, I remain compassionate and dedicated to the imperative of supporting the growth of human potential. This project was centered on exploring how we may support and build upon the capacity of our leaders who are charged with the immeasurable task of building teacher capacity as it connects to changing learning outcomes for our students. Therefore, I have elected to make the first mistake that Reeves proposed. I felt compelled to explore the prospect of a paradigm that may facilitate the "enactment of vital educational changes" (Reeves, 2009) as we cultivate a collective understanding for how to support our principals in the context of continuous reforms.

BIBLIOGRAPHY

Adelman, H. S., & Taylor, L. (2007). *Systemic change for school improvement*: Los Angeles: University of California, Los Angeles

Adelman, H. S., & Taylor, L. (2007). Systemic change for school improvement. *Journal of Educational and Psychological Consultation, 17*(1), 55–77.

Altieri, J. L. (2010). Cohort collaboration: School district, university collaborate to create tightly bonded group of graduate students. *Reading Today, 27*(6), 45.

Anderson-Butcher, D., Lawson, H. A., Iachini, A., Bean, G., Flaspohler, P. D., & Zullig, K. (2010). Capacity-related innovations resulting from the implementation of a community collaboration model for school improvement. *Journal of Educational and Psychological Consultation, 20*, 257–287. doi: 10.1080/10474412.2010.500512

Anfara, V., Jr., & Mertz, N. (2006). *Theoretical frameworks in qualitative research*. Thousand Oaks, CA: Sage.

Anglin, L. W., Mooradian, P. W., & Hoyt, D. L. (1992). Institutional renewal through professional development partnerships. *Community College Review, 19*(4), 52–56.

Beatty, B. (2007). Going through the emotions: Leadership that gets to the heart of school renewal. *Australian Journal of Education, 51*, 328–340.

Bender, W. (2009). *Beyond the RtI pyramid: Solutions for the First Years of Implementation*. Bloomington, IN: Solution Tree Press.

Birrell, J. R., Ostlund, M. R., Egan, M. W., Young, J. R., Cook, P. F., DeWitt, P. F., et al. (1998). Collaborations, communities and covey: A model for personal and professional change. *The Clearing House, 71*, 359–362. Retrieved January 17, 2013, from http://www.jstor.org/discover/10.2307/30189400?uid=3739816&uid=2&uid=4&uid=3739256&sid=21101946693947

Bolman, L. G., & Deal, T. (2002). *Reframing the path to school leadership: A guide for teachers and principals*. Thousand Oaks, CA: Corwin Press.

Booth, D., & Rowsell, J. *The literacy principal: Leading, supporting, and assessing reading and writing initiatives*. Portland, ME: Pembroke.

Browne-Ferrigno, T. (2011). Mandated university-district partnerships for principal preparation: Professors' perspectives on required program redesign. *Journal of School Leadership, 21*(5), 735–756.

Browne-Ferrigno, T., & Allen, L. W. (2006). Preparing principals for high-need rural schools: A central office perspective about collaborative efforts to transform school leadership. *Journal of Research in Rural Education, 21*(1), 1–16.

Browne-Ferrigno, T., & Sanzo, K. L. (2011). Introduction to special issue on university-district partnerships. *Journal of School Leadership, 21*, 650–658.

Buffum, A., Mattos, M., & Weber, C. (2009). *Pyramid response to intervention: RtI, professional learning communities, and how to respond when kids don't learn*. Bloomington, IN: Solution Tree.

Burbank, M. D., Bertagnole, H., Carl, S., Longhurst, T., Powell, K., & Dynak, J. (2005). University-district partnerships and recruitment of tomorrow's teachers: A grassroots effort for preparing quality educators through a teaching academy. *Teacher Education, 41*(1), 54–6.

Cadeau, K. M. (2011). Bridging the gap between middle school and university through Partnership: A reflection. *Journal of Multidisciplinary Research, 3*(3), 147–151.

Carr, J., Herman, N., & Harris, D. (2005). *Creating dynamic schools through mentoring, coaching, and collaboration*. Alexandria, VA: Association for Supervision and Curriculum Development (ASCD).

Darling-Hammond, L., & McLaughlin, M. W. (1995). Policies that support professional development in an era of reform. *Phi Delta Kappan, 76*, 597–604.

Darling-Hammond, L., Hightower, A., Husbands, J., Lafors, J., Young, V., & Christopher, C. (2005). *Instructional leadership for systemic change: The story of San Diego's reform*. Lanham, MD: Scarecrow Education.

Davis, S. H., & Darling-Hammond, L. (2012). Innovative principal preparation programs: What works and how we know. *Planning and Changing, 43*(1/2), 25–45.

BIBLIOGRAPHY

Doolittle, G., Sudeck, M., & Rattigan, P. (2008). Creating professional learning communities: The work of professional development schools. *Theory Into Practice, 47,* 303–310. DOI: 10.1080/00405840802329276

DuFour, R., DuFour, R., & Eaker, R. (2008). *Revisiting professional learning communities at work: New insights for improving schools.* Bloomington, IN: Solution Tree Press.

DuFour, R., DuFour, R., Eaker, R., & Karhanek, G. (2010). *Raising the bar and closing the gap: Whatever it takes.* Bloomington, IN: Solution Tree Press.

DuFour, R., DuFour, R., Eaker, & R., Many, T. (2006). *Learning by doing: A handbook for professional learning communities at work.* Bloomington, IN: Solution Tree Press

DuFour, R., DuFour, R., Eaker, R., Many, T., Marzano, R. Mattos, M., Muhammed, A., Reeves, D., & Williams, K. (2011). *Professional learning communities at work summit: New insights for improving schools.* Bloomington, IN: Solution Tree Press.

DuFour, R., & Marzano, R. (2011). *Leaders of learning: How district, school, and classroom leaders improve student achievement.* Bloomington, IN: Solution Tree Press.

Eaker, R., DuFour, & Burnette, R. (2002). *Getting started: Reculturing schools to become professional learning communities.* Bloomington, IN: National Education Service.

Enthoven, M., & Bruijn, E. d. (2010). Beyond locality: The creation of public practice-based knowledge through practitioner research in professional learning communities and communities of practice. A review of three books on practitioner research and professional communities. *Educational Access Research, 18,* 289–298. DOI: 10.1080/09650791003741822

Evans, R. (2001). The *human side of school change.* . San Francisco, CA: Jossey-Bass.

Fullan, M. (2001). *The new meaning of educational change.* New York, NY: Teachers College Press.

Fullan, M. (2005).The New Meaning of Educational Change (2005) Teachers College Columbia University

Fullan, M. (2008). *The six secrets of change.* San Francisco, CA: Jossey-Bass.

Gemberling, K., Smith, C., & Villani, J. (2009). *The key work of school boards: A guidebook.* Alexandria, VA: National School Boards Association (NSBA).

Getkin, K. (2009). Reforming or changing educational leadership. *The Journal for Quality and Participation, 32*(2), 15–19.

Glickman, C., Gordon, S., & Ross-Gordon, J. (2010, 2004, 2001, 1998, 1995, 1990, 1985). *SuperVision: And instructional leadership A developmental approach.* Boston, MA: Pearson Education.

Goldring, E., & Sims, P. (2005). Modeling creative and courageous school leadership through district-community-university partnerships. *Educational Policy, 19,* 223–249.

Gooden, M. A., Bell, C. M., Gonzales, R. M., & Lippa, A. P. (2011). Planning university-urban district partnerships: implications for principal preparation programs. *Educational Planning, 20*(2), 1–13.

Goodman, J. (1995). Change without difference: School restructuring in historical perspective. *Harvard Educational Review, 65*(1), 1–29.

Gorton, R., & Alston, J. (2009). *School leadership and administration: Important concepts, case studies, & simulations.* New York, NY: McGraw-Hill.

Graham, P., & Ferriter, W. M. (2010). Building a professional learning community at work: A guide to the first year. Foreword by Richard DuFour and Rebecca DuFour. Bloomington, IN: Solution Tree Press.

Guskey, T. (2000). *Evaluating professional development.* Thousand Oaks, CA: Corwin Press.

Hall, S. (2008). *A principal's guide: Implementing response to intervention.* Thousand Oaks, CA: Corwin Press.

Haretos, C. (2005). The No Child Left Behind Act of 2001: Is the definition of "adequate yearly progress" adequate? *Kennedy School Review, 6,* 29–46.

Hargreaves, A., & Fink, D. (2003, December). *The seven principles of sustainable leadership.* Retrieved http://www.marylandpublicschools.org

Heichberger, R. L. (1975). Creating the climate for humanistic change in the elementary school with principal as change agent. *Education, 96*(2), 106–112.

Hess, F. M., & Petrilli, M. J. (2004). The politics of No Child Left Behind: Will the coalition hold? *The Journal of Education, 185*(3), 13–25.

Hess, F.M., & Petrilli, M. J. (2011) The politics of No Child Left Behind: Will the coalition hold? *Educational Planning, 20,* (2011) 20(2)

150

BIBLIOGRAPHY

Hochberg, E. D., & Desimone, L. M. (2010). A professional development in the accountability context: Building capacity to achieve standards. *Educational Psychologist, 45*(2), 89–106. DOI: 10.1080/00461521003703052

Hoffman, J. N. (2004). Building resilient leaders: Many universities and school districts are creating support mechanisms that increase administrator resiliency and lead to greater retention. *Leadership, 34*(1), 35–39.

Holcomb, E. (1998). *Getting excited about data*. Thousand Oaks, CA: Corwin Press.

Holcomb, E. (2004). *Getting excited about data: Combining people, passion, and proof to maximize student achievement*. Thousand Oaks, CA: Corwin Press.

Hord, S. & Sommers, W. (2008). *Leading professional learning communities: Voices from research and practice*. Thousand Oaks, CA: Corwin Press.

Kaagan, S., & Headley, L. (2010). *Bringing your learning community to life: A road map for sustainable school improvement*. Thousand Oaks, CA: Corwin Press.

Korach, S. (2011). Keeping the fire burning: The evolution of a university-district collaboration to develop leaders for second-order change. *Journal of School Leadership, 21*, 659–683.

Kutash, J., Nico, E., Gorin, E., Rahmatullah, S., & Tallant, K. (2010, September). The Wallace Foundation. *The school turnaround field guide*, 1–62. Retrievable at http://www.wallacefoundation.org/knowledge-center/school-leadership/district-policy-and-practice/Documents/The-School-Turnaround-Field-Guide.pdf

Lambert, L. (1998). *Building leadership capacity in schools*. Alexandria, VA: Association for Supervision and Curriculum Development (ASCD).

Lane, K. L., Oakes, W. P., & Cox, M. (2011). Functional assessment-based interventions: A university-district partnership to promote learning and success. *Beyond Behavior, 20*(3), 3–18.

Ledoux, M. W., & McHenry, N. (2008). Pitfalls of school-university partnerships. *Clearing House: A Journal of Educational Strategies, Issues and Ideas, 81*(4), 155–160.

Leithwood, K., & Seashore Louis, K. (2012). *Linking leadership to student learning*. San Francisco, CA: Jossey-Bass.

Linn, R. L. (2010). A new era of test-based educational accountability. *Measurement: Interdisciplinary Research and Perspectives, 8*(2–3), 145–149. DOI: 10.1080/15366367.2010.508692

Ludeke (2011). Southwest District-Alliance Partnership. *The Alliance Newsletter*. New Mexico State University.

Lujan, M., Collins, B., & Love, S. (2008). *Master instructional strategies*. Mentoring Minds, LP: The Critical Thinking Source.

Lujan, M., Collins, B., Love, S., & Guerra, R., Jr. (2008). *Response to intervention (RtI) strategies*. Mentoring Minds LP: The Critical Thinking Source.

Lynch, J. M. (2012). Responsibilities of today's principal: Implications for principal preparation programs and principal certification policies. *Rural Special Education Quarterly, 31*(2), 40–47.

Marzano, R., & Waters, T. (2009). *District leadership that works: Striking the right balance*. Bloomington, IN: Solution Tree Press.

Matthews, L. J., & Crow, G. (2003). *Being and becoming a principal: Role conceptions for contemporary principals and assistant principals*. Boston, MA: Pearson Education.

Matthews, L. J., & Crow, G. (2010). *The principalship: New roles in a professional learning community*. Boston, MA: Pearson Education publishing as Allyn & Bacon.

McCaughtry, N., Krause, J., McAuliffe, P., Miotke, R., & Price, F. (2012). Detroit healthy youth initiative: Creating successful school-university partnerships. *Journal of Physical Education, Recreation and Dance, 83*(9), 28–36.

McDougall, D., Saunders, W. M., & Goldenberg, C. (2007). Inside the black box of school reform: Explaining the how and why of change at Getting Results schools. *International Journal of Disability, Development, and Education, 54*(1), 51–89.

McLaughlin, M. (2009). *What every principal needs to know about special education*. Thousand Oaks, CA: Corwin Press

Merriam, S. (1998). *Qualitative research and case study applications in education*. San Francisco, CA: A Jossey-Bass.

BIBLIOGRAPHY

Miller, T., Devin, M., & Shoop, R. (2007). *Closing the leadership gap: How district & university partnerships shape effective school leaders.* Thousand Oaks, CA: Corwin Press.

Moss, C., & Brookhart, S. (2009). *Advancing formative assessment in every classroom: A guide for instructional leaders.* Alexandria, VA: ASCD.

Mullen, C. A., & Hutinger, J. L. (2008). The principal's role in fostering collaborative learning communities through faculty study group development. *Theory into practice, 47,* 276–285. doi: 10.1080/00405840802329136

Myran, S., Sanzo, K. L., & Clayton, J. (2011). Tracing the development of a rural university-district partnership: Encouraging district voice and challenging assumptions leadership. *Journal of School Leadership, 21,* 684–703.

National Association of Elementary School Principals (NAESP) in Partnership with Collaborative Communications Group. (2008). *Leading learning communities: Standards for what principals should know and be able to do.* Alexandria, Virginia: National Association of Elementary School Principals (NAESP).

National Association of Elementary School Principals. (2012). *Rethinking principal evaluation: A new paradigm informed by research and practice.* Retrievable at http://www.nassp.org/Content/158/eval_report.PDF

National Conference of State Legislatures. (2008). A report to the legislative education study committee. *Strong leaders for New Mexico Schools Senate Joint Memorial 3: Report & Recommendations,* 1–25. Retrievable at http://www.ncsl.org/documents/educ/ NMSchoolLeaderTaskForceReport2008.pdf

Ontario Principals' Council. (2009). *The principal as professional learning community leader.* Thousand Oaks, CA: Corwin Press.

Orr, M. T., & Barber, M. E. (2006). Collaborative leadership preparation: A comparative study of partnership and conventional programs and practices. *Journal of School Leadership, 16,* 709–739.

Pace, D., & Burton, D. T. (2003). Professional development: Starting university district partnerships. *Academic Exchange, 7,* 292–298.

Papalewis, R., & Fortune, R. (2002). *Leadership on purpose: Promising practices for African American and Hispanic students.* Thousand Oaks, CA: Corwin-Press.

Porter, A. C., Goldring, E., Murphy, J., Elliott, S. N., & Cravens, X. (2006). The Wallace Foundation. *A framework for the assessment of learning-centered leadership,* 1–7. Retrievable at http://www.wallacefoundation.org/knowledge-center/school-leadership/principal-evaluation/Documents/A-Framework-for-the-Assessment-of-Learning-Centered-Leadership.pdf

Portin, B. S., Alejano, C. R., Knapp, M. S., & Marzolf, E. (2006). Redefining roles, responsibilities, and authority of school leaders. *Center for the Study of Teaching and Policy. University of Washington.,* 1–45. Retrievable at http://depts.washington.edu/ctpmail/PDFs/Roles-Oct16.pdf

Reardon, R. M. (2011). Elementary school principals' learning-centered leadership and educational outcomes: Implications for principals' professional development. *Leadership and Policy in Schools, 10*(1), 63–83. doi: 10/1080/15700760903511798

Reed, C. J., & Llanes, J. R. (2010). Raising standards for tomorrow's principals: Negotiating state requirements, faculty interests, district needs, and best practices. *Journal of Research and Leadership Education, 5,* 391–417.

Reeves, D. B. (2009). *Leading change in your school. How to conquer myths, build commitment, and get results.* Alexandria, VA: Association for Supervision and Curriculum Development (ASCD).

Reinhartz, J., & Beach, D. (2004). *Educational leadership: Changing schools, changing roles.* Boston, MA: Pearson Education.

Richmond, G., & Manokore, V. (2011). Identifying elements critical for functional and sustainable professional learning communities. *Science Education, 95,* 543–570. Retrieved January 17, 2013, from http://onlinelibrary.wiley.com/ doi/10.1002/sce.20430/abstract

Robinson, V. (2011). *Student-centered leadership.* San Francisco, CA: Jossey-Bass.

Rowland, B. (2005). Grounded in practice: Using interpretive research to build theory. *The Electronic Journal of Business Research Methodology 3.1,* 81–92. Print.

Rubin, H. (2002). *Collaborative leadership: Developing effective partnerships in communities and schools.* Thousand Oaks, CA: Corwin Press

BIBLIOGRAPHY

Rust, T. (2012). Technology and engineering education and the common core standards. *Technology and Engineering Teacher: The Voice of Technology and Engineering, 72*(3), 32–36.

Salazar, P. (2008). *High impact leadership for high impact schools: The actions that matter most.* Larchmont, NY: Eye on Education.

Sergiovanni, T. (2006). *The principalship: A reflective practice perspective.* Boston, MA: Pearson Education.

Sergiovanni, T. J. (2009) *The principalship: A reflective practice perspective.* Boston, MA: Pearson Education.

Shaw, P. (2012). *Taking charge: Leading with passion and purpose in the principalship.* New York, NY: Teachers College Press.

Shroyer, G., Yahnke, S., Bennett, A., & Dunn, C. (2007). Simultaneous renewal through professional development school partnerships. *Journal of Educational Research, 100*, 211–225.

Sigurðardóttir, A. K. (2010). Professional learning community in relation to school effectiveness. *Scandinavian Journal of Education Research, 54*, 395–412. DOI: 10.1080/00313831.2010.508904

Sindelar, P. T., Shearer, D. K., Yendol-Hoppey, D., & Liebert, T. W. (2006). The sustainability of inclusive school reform. *Exceptional Children, 72*, 317–331. http://www.wallacefoundation.org/knowledge-center/school-leadership/district-policy-and-practice/Documents/leading-change-handbook.pdf

Snider, E., O'Neill, K., & Gray, S. (2007). SREB leadership curriculum modules: Engaging leaders in solving real school problems--curriculum framework and module summaries. *Southern Regional Educational Board (SREB)*, 1–50. Retrievable at http://illinoisschoolleader.org/useful_resources/documents/SREB20Leadership20Curriculum20Modules.pdf

Southern Regional Education Board. (2012). Progress over a decade in preparing more effective school principles. Retrievable at http://publications.sreb.org/ 2012/12V17_ProgressOver_a_Decade_Benchmark.pdf

Spector, B. (2013, 2010, 2007). *Implementing organizational change: Theory into practice.* Upper Saddle River, NJ: Pearson Education.

Spillane, J. P., Healey, K., & Parise, L. M. (2009). School leaders' opportunities to learn: A descriptive analysis from a distributed perspective. *Educational Review, 61*, 407–432. DOI: 10:1080/0013191090340303998

Spiro, J. (2009). Leading change handbook: Concepts and tools. Retrievable at http://www.wallacefoundation.org/knowledge-center/school-leadership/district-policy-and-practice/Documents/leading-change-handbook.pdf

Stein, S., & Gewirtzman, L. (2003). *Principal training on the ground: Ensuring highly qualified leadership.* Portsmouth, NH: Heinemann.

Stevenson, C. B., Duran, R. L., Barrett, K. A., & Colarulli, G. C. (2005). Fostering faculty collaboration in learning communities: A developmental approach. *Innovative Higher Education, 30*(1), 23–36. doi: 10.1007/s10755-005-3293-3

Strier, R. (2011). The construction of university-community partnerships: Entangled perspectives. *Higher Education: The International Journal of Higher Education and Educational Planning, 62*(1), 81–97. doi: 100.1007/s10734-010-9367-x

Strong Leaders for New Mexico Schools: Senate Joint Memorial 3: Report & Recommendations. A report to the Legislative Education Study Committee. (2008, December). Prepared by P. Winograd, V. C. Garcia, & R. Dansenbrock.

Thompson, S. C., Gregg, L., & Niska, J. M. (2004). Professional learning communities, leadership, and student learning. *Research in Middle Level Education Online, 28*(1), 35–54. Retrieved January 17, 2013, from http://www.amle.org/ portals/0/pdf/publications/RMLE/rmlevol28no1article2.pdf

Villani, S. (2006). *Mentoring and induction programs that support new principals.* Thousand, Oaks, CA: Corwin Press.

Waldron, N. L., & McLeskey, J. (2010). Establishing a collaborative school culture through comprehensive school reform. *Journal of Education and Psychological Consultation, 20*, 58–74. doi: 10.1080/10474410903535364

The Wallace Foundation. (2002). *Searching for a superhero: Can principals do it all?* Education Writers Association, (Special Report). Retrieved from http://www.wallacefoundation.org/view-latest-news/InTheNews/ Documents/Searching-for-a-Superhero-Can-Principals-Do-It-All.pdf

BIBLIOGRAPHY

The Wallace Foundation. (2006). *Leadership for learning: Making the connections among state, district and school policies and practices.* Retrieved from http://www.wallacefoundation.org/knowledge-center/school-leadership/district-policy-and-practice/Documents/Wallace-Perspective-Leadership-for-Learning.pdf

The Wallace Foundation. (2010). *The three essentials: Improving schools requires district vision, district and state support, and principal leadership. Southern Regional Education Board.* Retrieved from http://www.wallacefoundation.org/ knowledge-center/school-leadership/district-policy-and-practice/Documents/ Three-Essentials-to-Improving-Schools.pdf

Warren, L. L., & Peel, H. A. (2005). Collaborative model for school reform through a rural school/university partnership. *Education, 126,* 346–352.

Weerts, D. J. (2005). Validating institutional commitment to outreach at land-grant universities: Listening to the voices of community partners. *Journal of Extension, 43*(5), 1–9. Retrieved January 30, 2013, from http://www.joe.org/joe/2005October/a3.php

Wiburg, K., & Brown, S. (2007). *Lesson study communities: Increasing achievement with diverse students.* Thousand Oaks, CA: Corwin Press.

Woolfolk Hoy, A., & Kolter Hoy, W. (2006). *Instructional leadership: A research-based guide to learning in schools.* Boston, MA: Pearson Education.

Yin, R. (2012). *Applications of case study research.* Thousand Oaks, CA: Sage.

Young, M. D. (2009). Research utilization briefs: University-district partnerships. *University Council for Educational Administration,* 1–2. Retrievable at http://ucea.org/storage/rub/ResearchUtilizationDec1509.pdf

Young, M. D. (2010). From the director: The promise of university-district partnerships. *University Council for Educational Administration, 51*(1), 1–3.

CPSIA information can be obtained at www.ICGtesting.com
Printed in the USA
LVOW08s2145290814

401611LV00004B/6/P

9 789462 093188